Key Words in Buddhism

Ron Geaves

Georgetown University Press / Washington, D.C.

As of January 1, 2007, 13-digit ISBN numbers will replace the current
10-digit system.
Paperback: 978-1-58901-129-8

Georgetown University Press, Washington, D.C.

Library of Congress Cataloging-in-Publication Data

Geaves, Ron.
  Key words in Buddhism / Ron Geaves.
      p. cm.
  ISBN 1-58901-129-5 (alk. paper)
  1. Buddhism—Dictionaries. I. Title.
  BQ130.G43 2006
  294.303—dc22
                              2006006891

This book is printed on acid-free paper meeting the requirements of the
American National Standard for Permanence in Paper for Printed Library
Materials.

13 12 11 10 09 08 07 06   9 8 7 6 5 4 3 2
First printing

Printed in Great Britain

Contents

PREFACE

During the course of teaching a number of religions in four higher
education institutions, one common feature has been the number of
students who have told me that they found the mastering of religious
terminology in so many unknown languages and involving unfamiliar
concepts to be the most daunting part of the module. In view of this, the
Key Words series was created to provide a glossary of terms for five
religions.

The religions have been chosen to reflect the main traditions that are
studied both in school and at university in the English-speaking world.
One glossary also contains the key specialist terminology used in the
academic study of religion. It is hoped that the glossaries will prove to
be useful and informative resources for anyone studying religion up to
undergraduate level, but that they will also provide a fascinating pool
of information for anyone interested in religious practice or belief,
whether for the purpose of gaining qualifications or simply in the
personal pursuit of knowledge. Each glossary therefore provides an
exhaustive exploration of religious terminology in a way that is acces-
sible but also provides an overall in-depth understanding of the religious
tradition.

Although Buddhism is now provided with its own separate book,
even so the glossary's completion remains arbitrary, as each religion
covered by the *Key Words* series commands a vast vocabulary that is a
conceptual framework for viewing the world. This is especially true of
Buddhism, which is a fully developed religious tradition over 2,500 years
old and represents considerable religious diversity and a global reach
from Japan to Europe, with minority communities in North and South
America and Australasia. As Buddhism spread through Asia it assimi-
lated several local religions and developed various forms unique to
diverse cultures such as Japan, China and Tibet. It virtually disappeared
in its place of origin, but the Indian languages of Pali and Sanskrit

remain significant for the textual canons of the Theravada and Mahayana traditions. However, Japan and China in particular developed their own forms of Buddhism with specialist terminology in their respective languages. My choice of terms has been determined by school and undergraduate curricula, and the length of each definition has been dictated by the fact that this is a glossary and not a specialist religious dictionary. Inevitably, however, some concepts and persons needed more than a short passage in order to clarify their significance and highlight their importance within the world of their respective religion. I have also decided to transliterate the terms into the English alphabet without diacritics. Although this may irritate the specialist scholar, especially those whose work is textual study, it remains part of the spirit of the original *Continuum Glossary of Religious Terms*, which was to provide acceptable variant spellings to non-specialists. The main variants are Pali or Sanskrit, but Japanese, Tibetan and Chinese terms are included. The code for the languages is as follows:

Ch	Chinese
J	Japanese
P	Pali
S	Sanskrit
T	Tibetan

Finally, I would like to thank Catherine Barnes, whose patience and support has been remarkable; Janet Joyce, who provided the original opportunity for this project to grow from its inception to completion; and Continuum for providing the means for the glossaries to appear in their various editions.

Abhidhamma (P) / Abhidharma (S)   The philosophy and psychology of Buddhism presented in an abstract systematic form as a 'higher' or 'further' exposition of the Buddha's teachings. The Abhidhamma literature consists of commentaries and interpretations of the earliest SUTRAS and provides a systematic analysis of the Buddha's discourses. Generally they are concerned with the analysis of the totality of existence, dividing it into building blocks from which human beings construct their lived reality. (*See also* ADHIDHAMMA PITAKA; DHAMMAS)

Abhidhamma Pitaka (P) / Abhidharma Pitaka (S)   *Lit. basket of higher teachings.* The third section of the canon of scripture belonging to the THERAVADA tradition consisting of seven texts arranged by the Buddha's early followers. It is an abstract and impersonal philosophical treatise concerned with psychical and mental phenomena which was extracted and systematized from the basic teachings of the Buddha. The texts function as a series of commentaries and are believed by some to be the words of the Buddha. Two complete Abhidharma Pitakas survive in the present: the Theravadins of South-East Asia and the SARVASTIVADINS of North-West India. However, the Sarvastivadins always acknowledged that the works were compiled by various authors, whereas the Theravadins insisted they were the works of the Buddha. The Sarvastivadin collections now only survive in Tibetan and Chinese versions. There are seven books in each collection: The Theravada collection consists of the *Dhammasangani*, *Vibhanga*, *Dhatukatha*, *Puggalapannati*, *Kathuvatthu*, *Yamaka* and the *Patthana*. The Sarvastivadin collection consists of the

Jnanaprasthana, Prakaranapada, Vijnanakaya, Dharmaskandha, Prajnaptisastra, Dhatukaya and the *Sangitiparyaya*. (*See also* TIPITAKA)

Abhidharmakosa   A non-Mahayanan text concerned with the understanding and discernment of the dhammas, attributed to Vasabandhu, the brother of ASANGA. In Tibet, the Sanskrit version of the text functions as the main vehicle for understanding the ABHIDHARMA.

Abhidharmasamuccaya   A sacred text of the MAHAYANA tradition that is attributed to ASANGA. The text constructs a Mahayana CITTAMATRA ABHIDHARMA and indicates that the Mahayana tradition was not completely in opposition to the Abhidharma.

Abhijna   *Lit. the higher knowledges.* The insight which came to the Buddha on the night of his enlightenment. There are three insights or knowledges: the opening of the divine eye; remembrance of past lives; and the extinction of the tendencies that lead to ignorance.

Abhirati   A Buddha field or PURE LAND said to exist in the distant east and the domain of the Buddha AKSOBHYA. It is described in the AKSOB-HYAVYUHA SUTRA as a place with no illness, deceit or ugliness, where trees are in bloom all year round. Food appears on request and all sentient beings live in joy practising the DHARMA. (*See also* BUDDAK-SHETRA)

Abhisamayalamkara   A Tibetan sacred text attributed to the future BODHISATTVA MAITREYA. Tibetans study the PRAJNAPARAMITRA through the medium of this text.

Adi   The doctrine of a primordial or eternally enlightened Buddha developed in the tenth century. However, this is generally refuted as it would lead to contradiction with the idea that all beings are given access to enlightenment through progress over successive lifetimes. (*See also* DHAMMAKAYA; TATHAGATAGHARBA; TRIKAYA).

Agama   *See* NIKAYA.

Agganna Sutta   A Theravadin SUTRA which documents the Buddha's criticisms of the Hindu caste system and his attitude to Brahmins. The tone is tongue-in-cheek and humorous but the function is to undermine the caste system and demonstrate that it is merely a human social convention.

Ahara   The condition or cause that maintains an object's existence. Materially it means nourishment, but the concept refers to four causes or conditions essential for the existence and continuity of beings. (*See also* KAHALINKARAHARA; MANOSANCETANAHARA; PASSAHARA; VINNANAHARA)

Ahimsa   *Ahimsa*, or harmlessness, is a central aspect of right livelihood in Buddhism, one of the aspects of the Noble Eightfold Path that leads to eventual freedom from SAMSARA. A practising Buddhist will refrain from anything that may cause harm to other living beings, a consideration that should influence the choice of occupation. (*See also* SAMMA AJIVA)

Ajitasena Sutra   A short SUTRA discovered in Afghanistan on the topic of giving alms to monks. It is very old and predates the MAHAYANA development in Buddhism. Its significance to Buddhist scholars is that it states early forms of doctrines that were to become significant to the fully developed Mahayana tradition, such as the progress to Buddhahood through many incarnations. (*See also* BODHISATTVA)

Aksobhya   Probably the earliest cult to a Buddha other than SIDDATTHA GOTTAMA. The Buddha Aksobhya is known through the AKSOBHYAVYUHA SUTRA. It is recounted in the *sutra* that he was a monk who made and fulfilled a number of stringent vows, especially in the realm of morality. These included never to bear enmity towards others, to be mindful in the company of women, never to listen to non-Buddhist doctrines, never to engage in immorality, and to save criminals about to be punished. The purity of the monk's vows, carried out for many lifetimes, allowed him to attain BODHISATTVA and then Buddhahood. In addition, the vows impacted upon the purity of his eventual Buddha field which was to become a PURE LAND. (*See also* ABHIRATI; BUDDHAKSHETRA)

Aksobhyavyuha Sutra   The SUTRA, originally written in the local dialect of Gandhari, a language of North-West India, was translated into Chinese in the second century CE and is one of the earliest of the MAHAYANA *sutras*. It is the main source of information on the cult and mythology of AKSOBHYA. (*See also* ABHIRATI)

Akusala (P)   *Lit. unwholesome.* Used to describe actions that bring about bad *karma* and consequently lead to bad rebirth. Philosophically it is used to describe desires which are accompanied by greed, hatred or delusion. (*See also* KAMMA; KUSALA)

Alaya-vijnana   A store of past *karma* maintained in the field of consciousness that is carried on to the next birth. This store contains the pure seeds of *karma* that will eventually awaken the desire to achieve enlightenment. (*See also* KAMMA; KUSALA)

Amida (J) / Amitabha (S)   The transcendent Buddha of Infinite Light or the Buddha of the Pure Realm; the personification of mercy, wisdom, love and compassion found in Chinese and Japanese Buddhism. The MAHAYANA belief that there were Buddhas who were teaching in other realms known as the PURE LAND gave rise to the East-Asian schools of Buddhism known as Pure Land sects. The unique feature of these movements was the aspiration to attain rebirth in the Pure Land made possible by repetition of the name of Amida Buddha. The Chinese BODHISATTVA named DHARMAKARA became the Japanese Amida Buddha central to the worship of the JODO school.

Amitayurbuddhanusmriti Sutra   A SUTRA supposedly translated into Chinese in the fifth century CE, concerned primarily with the visualization of Buddhas and *bodhisattvas*. The text is important to the AMIDA Buddhists as it contains a discourse between SAKYAMUNI Buddha and Queen Vaidehi in which the Buddha reveals to Vaidehi thirteen visualization meditations on AMIDA guaranteed to gain access to his PURE LAND. The *sutra* promises access to even the greatest sinner and it is upon this teaching that the Amida Buddhists base their devotional doctrines of salvation. (*See also* BUDDHANUSMRTI; BODHISSATVA)

Amitayus   *See* AMIDA.

Anagarika   *Lit. homeless.* A title used by Dharmapala, a famous nineteenth-century Sinhalese nationalist and Buddhist revivalist. Dharmapala created the anagarika as an intermediate status between the laity and the monks. He wore a white robe but did not shave his head, and espoused a life of chastity and abstinence. He took a vow of obedience to the eight precepts normally only obeyed by the laity on feast days. However, since the politicization of Sri Lankan Buddhism, many monks are politically active and many members of the laity are practising ascetics, thus the formal status of anagarika has become less popular.

Anapanasati (P) / Anapanasmrti (S)   *Lit. awareness of the in-and-out breathing.* Mindfulness or meditation on the breath which is one of the most common forms of Buddhist meditation. It is a practice that is always done sitting in posture, or least with an erect spine, and is usually associated with developing concentration and calm. It is important in developing VIPASSANA. It is believed in some traditions that Buddha SAKYAMUNI attained enlightenment by this means.

Anatta (P) / Anatman (S)   The concept that there is no permanent self or ego and that everything in SAMSARA is in a condition of insubstantiality or impermanence. The denial of a permanent self or soul is unique to Buddhism amongst religions of Indian origin, and debates have taken place as to whether or not Buddha denied the existence of a permanent self. What is not in doubt is the fact that the self described by the Buddha was formed of various aggregates that would eventually separate into their various components. However, when asked by his disciple Ananda whether the self was permanent or impermanent, he is recorded as refusing to answer on the grounds that he did not wish to enter into doctrinal disputes. Certainly, according to traditional Buddhist teaching, it is one of the three signs of illusionary being, and the belief that there is a permanent ego or soul will ensure that suffering continues as a characteristic of transitory existence. (*See also* ANICCA; ATA; DUKKHA)

Angulimaliya Sutra   A Tibetan SUTRA which teaches that Manjushri, the BODHISATTVA who is the incarnation of wisdom, already has a Buddha field of his own and is therefore a Buddha. (*See also* BUDDHAKSHETRA; MANJUSHRI)

Anicca (P) / Anitya (S)   The second of the three signs of being which constitute the continuation of SAMSARA. Anicca is the continuing flux of all matter, states of mind or consciousness and describes the important doctrine of the impermanence of all things. (*See also* ANATTA; DUKKHA)

Anupassana   The attention or observation required by the practitioner in meditation in order to attain mindfulness or awareness. (*See also* VIPASSANA)

Appamada   *Lit. diligence.* The Buddha refers to diligence not in the sense of hard work but rather awareness or attentiveness. Such attention to the details of existence may involve virtues of thrift.

Apramana (S) / Appamana (P)   A form of meditation known as the four sublime states in which the practitioner tries to achieve unlimited universal love for all beings, compassion for everything that is suffering, sympathetic joy for the happiness and success of others, and equanimity in the all the ups and downs of existence. These states are also known as BRAHMA VIHARAS. (*See also* KARUNA; METTA; MUDITA; UPEKKHA)

Aramika   A lay attendant to a monk or a monastery.

Arhant / Arahunt (P) / Arhat (S)   An enlightened disciple or one who has attained enlightenment. The *arhant* is believed to be free from all craving and desire for rebirth and has attained the state of NIRVANA. It is the ideal goal in the THERAVADA tradition of Buddhism and used to describe the Buddha and the highest level of his disciples. In the MAHAYANA tradition, it describes one who enters Nirvana but selfishly does not remain in the BODHISATTVA condition. (*See also* BUDDHA)

Ariyatthangikamagga   The Noble Eightfold Path taught by the Buddha as the skilful means or middle way to obtain release from suffering. It consists of Right Understanding, Right Thought, Right Speech, Right Action, Right Livelihood, Right Effort, Right Mindfulness and Right Concentration. (*See also* SAMMA AJIVA; SAMMA DITTHI; SAMMA KAMMANTA; SAMMA SAMADHI; SAMMA SATI; SAMMA VACA; SAMMA VAYAMA)

Arupadhatu   The domain of formless, superhuman activity and one of three layers or realms of existence that make up the world system in Buddhist cosmology. It is the highest meditative world which is achieved by the Buddhas before final enlightenment and NIRVANA and gives rise to the MAHAYANA doctrines of the PURE LAND, or the realms where the Buddhas teach. (*See also* AMIDA; AVACARA; KAMADHATU; RUPADHATU)

Asaiksamarga   The Path of No More Learning, which according to the BHAVANAKRAMAS, is the final stage in the development of a BODHISATTVA, when one enters the state of complete Buddhahood from which there is no coming back. (*See also* BHAVANAMARGA; DARSANAMARGA; PRAYOGAMARGA; SAMBHARAMARGA)

Asanga   (310–90 CE). A well-known Tibetan who struggled to achieve the vision of MAITREYA, the future Buddha. The story states that he finally succeeded when he helped a starving dog by the roadside. The dog was none other than Maitreya himself, who can only be seen in moments of great compassion. It is said that Maitreya revealed five sacred texts to Asanga; the *Abhisamayalamkara*, the 'Perfection of Wisdom'; the *Madhyantavibhaga*, the 'Discrimination of the Middle from Extremes'; the *Dharmadharmatavibhaga*, the 'Discrimination of Dharmas and their True Nature'; the *Mahayanasutralamkara*, 'The Ornament of the Mahayana Sutras'; and the *Ratnagotravibhaga*, a treatise on Buddha essences.

Asavas   The four mental defilements which delude the mind and prevent enlightenment. (*See also* AVIJJA; BHAVA; DITTHI; KAMA)

7

Asoka (P) / Ashoka (S)   The ruler of the kingdom of Magadha in Northern India (273–32 BCE). He embraced Buddhism after his conquest of the kingdom of Kalinga in which he experienced deep remorse at the level of bloodshed. He met with many monks but tradition states that his conversion took place after meeting the monk Nigodha. Ashoka adopted AHIMSA or non-violence and based his administration on Buddhist DHAMMA. He was highly influential in the spread of Buddhist teachings throughout his dominions in India and South-East Asia.

Asokadattavyakarana Sutra   A *sutra* used by MAHAYANA traditions to support their doctrines concerning the significance of the Buddhist laity and women and their ability to attain the same levels of enlightenment as the monks. The *sutra* demonstrates this doctrinal position by recounting the story of Asokadatta, a twelve-year-old princess who refused to stand and make obeisance to monks who had entered her father's palace. She argues that she has entered upon the path of the BODHISATTVA and is therefore superior to monks who are only on the path to being ARHANTS. In addition, she suggests that the monks' attitudes towards the spiritual inferiority of women indicates that they are trapped inside dualistic thinking. (*See also* BHADRA-MAYAKARAVYAKARANA SUTRA VIMALAKAKIRTINIRDESA SUTRA)

Astadasasahasrika   The 18,000-verse text which along with the *Satasahasrika* (100,000 verses) and the *Pancavimsatisahasrika* (25,000 verses) forms one of the categories of PRAJNAPARAMITA literature in the Mahayana canon. (*See also* PANNA)

Astasahasrika   The 8,000-verse text translated as the *Perfection of Wisdom* which is the oldest MAHAYANA PRAJNAPARAMITA SUTRA. (*See also* PANNA)

Atta (P) / Atman (S)   The Self or soul which in Buddhist teaching refers to the illusory ego or self-identity. Belief in its permanence is responsible for bondage to SAMSARA. It is not believed to be permanent as the *atman* in Hindu teaching. (*See also* ANATTA)

Avacara One of the three spheres of existence, KAMA, RUPA and ARUPA, in which all beings exist.

Avalokiteshwara A title used in MAHAYANA tradition for one of the greatest and most popular *bodhisattvas*. He is the '*Lord who is seen*', or '*the Lord who lowers his gaze towards humanity in mercy and compassion and the wish to help*'. The LOTUS SUTRA describes him as coming to the assistance of all who call on him, working tirelessly for the eradication of suffering. He not only removes lust, wrath and stupidity but grants children on request. He is believed to appear in any form that is necessary for the protection of his supplicants, whether monk, householder, human or non-human. Many Tibetans believe that the DALAI LAMA is a form of Avalokiteshwara, but in whatever guise he is venerated it is generally believed that he is one of the most powerful of *bodhisattvas*, full of compassion, a saviour who is concerned not only with enlightenment but also with the problems of daily life. In China worshipped as the feminine KUAN YIN, or KWANNON in Japan. (*See also* BODHISATTVA)

Avatamsaka Sutra Mahayana scripture which presents the doctrine of cosmic identity and forms the basis of the teachings of the HUA-YEN school. The idea of cosmic identity advocates that everything interpenetrates everything else so that ultimate truth may be perceived in a grain of dust. However, the SUTRA is written from the perspective of an advanced BODHISATTVA or Buddha. The text was probably translated into Chinese from the Sanskrit in the fifth century CE and some of the contents may have been added in Central Asia.

Avijja (P) / Avidya (S) *Lit. 'not knowing' or 'ignorance'*. Ignorance of the true nature of existence and the primary root of being trapped in the wheel of SAMSARA. It is the root of evil, the cause of desire and the first NIDANA or link in the causal chain of existence. It is also one of the four ASAVAS that create attachment. (*See also* KARUNA; METTA; MUDITA; UPEKKHA)

B

Bardo (T)   In Tibetan Buddhism, a series of intermediate states of being between death and rebirth where the consciousness-continuum faces powerful and sometimes terrifying apparitions according to the level of understanding and progress achieved in the former life. Rebirth is determined by the ability to deal with these phenomena. The precise nature of the Bardo experiences is laid out in the Tibetan Book of the Dead. (*See also* KAMMA)

Bhadramayakaravyakarana Sutra   A SUTRA used by Mahayana traditions to support their doctrines concerning the significance of the Buddhist laity and their ability to attain the same levels of enlightenment as the monks. The *sutra* demonstrates this doctrinal position by arguing that monks only renounce householder life whereas *bodhisattvas* are able to attain similar states of detachment whilst living in the midst of worldly activities. Thus a BODHISATTVA's goal is to attain true understanding of the nature of reality not merely to renounce the world. (*See also* ASOKA-DATTAVYAKARANA SUTRA; MAHAYANA; VIMALAKAKIRTINIRDESA SUTRA)

Bhaisajyaguru   Bhaisajyaguru is the Buddha of medicine. A significant figure in Tibet and China, he functions as the presiding Buddha over all healing activities, including enlightenment, the ultimate cure for the human condition. Monk-physicians, in particular, call upon him or meditate upon him to enhance their healing powers and his MANTRA is used to add to the efficacy of medicines. The sick can be saved by venerating the medicine Buddha. The qualities of this Buddha and his Buddha field are described in the BHAISAJYAGURU SUTRA.

Bhaisajyaguru Sutra   The SUTRA that decribes the qualities of the medicine Buddha and his realm. It also contains details for his correct veneration. It was probably first written in Sanskrit and then translated into Tibetan, although it is possible that the Tibetan version is the original as there is no evidence of a medicine-Buddha cult having existed in India. East Asian translations exist from the seventh century. The *sutra* describes the vows taken by the BODHISATTVA on his path to Buddhahood, one of which vows to cure all diseases in those who call upon the Buddha's name. Women who are tired of the female condition can also be reborn as men through the Buddha's supplication. The Buddha field or realm of the medicine Buddha is described as having no women or non-Mahayanan inhabitants. The Buddha is accompanied by two *bodhisattva* attendants, Suryaprabha and Candraprabha, who lead the dead into his presence. (*See also* BHAISAJYAGURU)

Bhaisajyaraja   A BODHISATTVA described in the LOTUS SUTRA as offering his body in a previous life as a perfect gift to the Buddha by burning it. The practice of body burning described in the scripture may have had some influence on the political sacrifices made by East-Asian monks in the contemporary period, especially as a protest against the Vietnam war.

Bhava   *Lit. becoming and rebecoming*. The longing for life that is the normal state of all living beings confined to samsara. It is one of the four ASAVAS that keep a human being in a condition of attachment and a link in the chain which keeps a being in the wheel of SAMSARA and maintains the cycle of rebirth. In the causal chain of existence *bhava* arises from UPADANA or clinging to existence. (*See also* JATI; NIDANAS)

Bhavana   The path of development which is divided into ordinary and transcendent attainments: ordinary attainment is the mastery of calm but the transcendent path involves complete loss of attachment, including even the fruits of meditation. (*See also* VIPASSANA)

Bhavanakramas   A set of three texts written in the eighth century CE by the Indian monk, Kamasila, an early missionary to Tibet, which function as the most influential Indian texts in Tibet for comprehending the stages on the path to enlightenment.

Bhavanamarga   The Path of Cultivation, which according to the BHAVANAKRAMAS is the fourth stage in the development of a BODHISATTVA, when one is possessed of perfectly pure morality consisting of abstaining from killing, theft and sexual misconduct, lying, slander, insults, frivolous speech, greed, hatred and false views. The *bodhisattva* can pass lifetimes in this stage practising morality in compassionate activity. (*See also* ASAIKSAMARGA; DARSANAMARGA; PRAYOGAMARGA; SAMBHARAMARGA)

Bhavanga   The mind that has achieved a state of rest in which it is free from the process of sense perception and reaction to sense perception. (*See also* BHAVANA)

Bhikku (P) / Bhikshu (S)   *Lit. one who begs food.* Although probably used at the time of the Buddha to describe all mendicants, he used it specifically as the title for a member of the Order of the SANGHA or a fully ordained Buddhist monk. Today it is used only to describe Buddhist monks rather than mendicants in general. (*See also* BHIKKUNI)

Bhikkuni (P) / Bhikshuni (S)   A fully ordained Buddhist nun. Although the Buddha ordained women into the Order of the SANGHA, it is believed that he insisted that they were always subordinate to a male monk regardless of age or duration in the Sangha. In most Buddhist countries the order of nuns has declined or even disappeared, although there are attempts to revitalize it. (*See also* BHIKKU)

Bhumi   The nine stages of the *bodhisattva* on the path to Buddhahood. First stage: known as the Joyous Stage, the *bodhisattva* becomes a Noble One or Arya where he/she attains control over future rebirths. Second stage: the Immaculate or Pure Stage where the *bodhisattva* achieves perfect morality. Third stage: the Luminous Stage where the perfection of patience is achieved and impermanance is completely understood. A light appears in meditation which burns away all duality and the *bodhisattva* is illuminated. Fourth stage: the Ignited or Radiant Stage where the *bodhisattva* ends all attachment to self and achieves the perfection of effort. Fifth stage: the Stage of Difficult to Conquer where the *bodhisattva* cannot be overcome by the powers of evil and achieves the perfection of meditation. Sixth stage: the Stage of Approaching where the *bodhisattva* achieves the perfection of wisdom. It at this point that the *bodhisattva* is faced with the choice of becoming an ARHANT and abandoning the world in perfect peace or to remain in the world for the benefit of other suffering beings. Seventh stage: the Stage of Gone Afar, the *bodhisattva* practises skilful means for the salvation of others, cultivating pleasant speech, impartiality and benevolent conduct. Eighth stage: the Immovable Stage, where the state of the *bodhisattva* cannot be reversed. There is no more striving even for enlightenment. Ninth stage: the Stage of Good Intelligence, where the knowledge and duties of all the enlightened beings are understood and the *bodhisattva* begins to deliver the Buddha's teachings to all sentient beings. Tenth stage: the Cloud of Dharma, where the *bodhisattva* mounts a celestial throne and emits rays of light which spread compassion towards all sentient beings. Beyond the tenth stage is the realm of the Buddha.

Bodh-Gaya   Town in the northern state of Bihar where the Buddha achieved enlightenment. It is named after the BODHI TREE where the Buddha sat whilst meditating before entering SAMADHI. It is now an important international Buddhist pilgrimage site containing temples built by Buddhist communities throughout the world.

Bodhi   Enlightenment or awakening. The spiritual condition of a Buddha, BODHISATTVA or an ARHANT which involves an understanding of the processes of suffering, the cause of suffering and the cessation of suffering through the application of the Eightfold Path. Various forms of Buddhism teach both gradual and sudden awakening. (*See also* BUDDHA; NIRVANA; SAMADHI; SATORI)

Bodhi Tree   (*Ficus Religiosa*) The tree under which the Buddha meditated and achieved enlightenment. Also known as the Tree of Wisdom. The original BODHI tree is believed to be in BODH-GAYA but offshoots were transplanted in Sri Lanka and Sarnath, the site of the Buddha's first sermon near Varanasi. All three are now major pilgrimage sites.

Bodhicitta   The Mind of Enlightenment or Awakening that constitutes the essential element of MAHAYANA Buddhism. It is the wisdom-filled heart of the BODHISATTVA that creates the motivation to seek rebirth in order to relieve the suffering of all sentient beings who remain trapped in SAMSARA.

Bodhidharma   The legendary Indian Buddhist monk who is believed to have founded the CH'AN school in China in the fifth or sixth century CE. Bodhidharma emphasized the teachings of the Lankavatara SUTRA which centres on reaching the 'emptiness' beyond all forms of conceptual thought. The Buddha nature within all beings is realized by sudden awakening. According to tradition, he transported Ch'an from China to Japan about 520 CE where it became ZEN.

Bodhipathapradipa   A text written by Atisa which divides beings into three types based upon their motivation. The lowest pursues the pleasures of the world; the middling pusues their own enlightenment for the selfish goal of their own peace of mind; whereas the highest seek to end the suffering of all sentient beings, in short the BODHISATTVA concept, central to MAHAYANA Buddhism.

Bodhisatta (P) / Bodhisattva (S)   A term used in MAHAYANA tradition for someone destined to become a Buddha through the development of BODHICITTA, but who renounces entry to NIRVANA in order to help other beings through compassion or empathy with their suffering. This compassion creates a deep resolve to assist others to become free from the wheel of SAMSARA. Thus the *bodhisattvas* postpone their own final entry into Nirvana in order to assist all sentient beings towards their spiritual goal. Many BODHISATTVAS are regarded as living in pure realms as supernatural beings, where they teach and assist sentient beings towards enlightenment. Mahayana Buddhists perform PUJA or veneration towards them in the hope of spiritual reward. Other BODHISATTVAS are human beings of great spiritual attainment. (*See also* AVALOKITESHVARA; BODHISATTVA; DALAI LAMA)

Bodhisattva Pitaka   An important MAHAYANA SUTRA that provides a detailed map of the stages required in becoming a BODHISATTVA.

Bodhisattva yana   The spiritual vehicle of the BODHISATTVA. The term given to the first followers or movement to declare the superiority of the BODHISATTVA ideal over the arhant. As the new movement defended itself against criticism it began to place emphasis on its superiority and thus became MAHAYANA.

Bodhisena An eighth-century Indian monk who helped to bring the HUA-YEN school of Buddhism from China to Japan where it was established as KEGON.

Bodhyangas A way of categorizing the Eightfold Path that emphasizes its cumulative nature. The bodhyangas refer to the stages of BODHI or awakening. It consists of seven stages, each dependent on full realization of the previous one. The first is SMRITI defined as awareness of the body, feelings and all mental activity; the second is specific awareness of mental states and the identification of those which are positive and conducive to spiritual life; the third stage is VIRIYA, or energy required to make the effort to cultivate the states of mind recognized at the second stage; the fourth is PRITI, or rapture which is the result of energy; the fifth is PRASRABDHI, a refined state of spiritual happiness in which awareness of physical surroundings is lessened and absorption in bliss occurs; the final stage is UPEKKHA, or equanimity, a state of deep tranquility and insight.

Bompu zen (J) The first of the five types of ZEN, known as 'Ordinary' Zen as opposed to the other four which are thought to be special and only suitable for particular types of individual or specialized intentions. (*See also* DAIJO; GEDO; SAIJOJO; SHOJO)

Brahmajala Sutra A MAHAYANA text which provides the ten major precepts and the forty-eight minor ones expected of those who embark on the BODHISATTVA path.

Brahma Viharas The four sublime states of loving kindness, compassion, sympathetic joy, and evenness of mind achieved by the practice of BHAVANA. (*See also* KARUNA; METTA; MUDITA; UPEKKHA)

Buddha A title meaning the enlightened or awakened one given to SIDDATTHA GOTTAMA after his enlightenment. The Mahayana tradition recognizes more than one Buddha as it believes that countless Buddhas have manifested out of the life principle throughout aeons of time. On the other hand, the THERAVADA tradition focuses on the historical Siddattha Gottama. Although the condition of a Buddha is also considered to have been achieved by his closest disciples and other ARHANTS throughout Buddhist history, it is the Buddhas who receive the veneration of Buddhists throughout the world. (*See also* ARHANT; BODHI; BODHISATTVA)

Buddha Nature *See* TATHAGATA GHARBA.

Buddha Pratima / Buddha Rupa An image or statue of the Buddha. They usually represent the Buddha as seated, standing or lying on his right side. There are many varieties used throughout the Buddhist world especially in the MAHAYANA tradition.

Buddhaghosa A monk sent from BODH-GAYA in the fourth century CE to Sri Lanka to bring the vast PALI CANON and its commentaries back to India. Buddhaghosa wrote most of the commentaries on the Canon, including the authoritative VISUDDHI-MAGGA, recognized by the THERAVADA.

Buddakshetra The Buddha fields or worlds where the Buddhas reside and teach. Buddhism acknowledges the existence of countless worlds and universes but Buddhas are relatively rare. There are worlds where no Buddhas teach or have influence and it is not possible for more than one Buddha to be present in a Buddha field.

Buddhanusmrti Recollection or remembrance of the Buddha in meditation. In the EKOTTARAGAMA, a canonical collection of the pre-MAHAYANA, there is a SUTRA which advocates that such recollection can lead to enlightenment.

Buddhavacana The actual words or discourses attributed to the Buddha.

C

Cakkavatti (P) / Chakravarti (S)   *Lit. turning of the wheel.* The concept of universal monarch. It was foretold at the Buddha's birth that he would either be a CAKKAVATTI or an enlightened Buddha who would rescue sentient beings from suffering. For this reason, his father tried to avoid contact with suffering, exposing the future Buddha to pleasure only, to try to determine his destiny as a CAKKAVATTIN not a Buddha. The term can also be used to indicate a significant turning of the wheel of *dhamma*, a new teaching or understanding of the Buddha's message that transforms human existence. (*See also* BUDDHA)

Cattari Ariyasaccani   The Four Noble Truths and the heart of Buddhist teaching concerning suffering, taught by the Buddha in his first sermon at VARANASI after achieving enlightenment, and delivered to the group of ascetics who had deserted him after he had left practising austerities. (*See also* DUKKHA; MAGGA; NIRODHA; SAMUDAYA)

Cettana   Volition or the will to live, to continue which functions as the root of existence that leads to rebirth by driving human beings towards good and bad actions. (*See also* MANOSANCETANAHARA)

Ch'an (Ch)   The Chinese pronunciation of DHYANA or JNANA, the Ch'an school is focused around direct experience in meditation and simple activity. It is opposed to discursive thinking as it considers it to be a hindrance on the path to awakening. Its origin is attributed to BODHID-HARMA but it acknowledges a lineage of masters each enlightened by direct transmission. The lineage began with MAHAKASYAPA who according to legend achieved enlightenment when he saw the Buddha silently holding a flower. The tradition believes in a sudden awakening that realizes the existence of the Buddha nature within. (*See also* ZEN).

Ching T'u (Ch)   A Chinese Buddhist school that stresses the essential place of 'other-power' in achieving enlightenment. Whereas CH'AN focuses on personal effort, Ching T'u refers to the effort made by the AMIDA Buddha to enlighten sentient beings. All practices of the school are oriented towards rebirth in the PURE LAND, SUKHAVATI, the domain of Amida. The main practice is repetition of the Buddha's name. Although there are other Amida schools in China, the Ching T'u was probably the first, arriving in the country in the second century CE.

Citta   Consciousness. The experience of being aware of something. However, in Buddhism, consciousness is an aggregate of associated mental factors such as contact, feeling, recognition, volition, one-pointedness and bringing-to-mind. Each combination that arises lasts for a short moment and is conscious of just one thing. Thus consciousness cannot be seen as the ground of our being or a constant, as in most Hindu philosophy.

Cittakaggata (P) / Cittakagrata (S)   One of the two forms of meditation that can lead to one-pointedness of mind and can be achieved by a variety of techniques and methods depending on the school or teacher. The Buddha taught that they pre-existed his life and therefore are not explicitly Buddhist. The other form of meditation is uniquely Buddhist. (*See also* VIPASSANA)

Cittamatra   The aspect of NIRVANA as Nothing-but-Thought as taught by the Yogicharin School. The proposition is that one can only know an experience of something with the mind. Cittamatra also refers to the Yogicharin School and the body of texts used by them, which frequently refer to the concept of the Buddha's three bodies. (*See also* TRIKAYA; YOGACARA)

D

Daijo zen (J)   The fourth of the five types of ZEN known as 'MAHAYANA' or 'Great Vehicle' Zen. The central teaching concerns seeing into one's essential nature and realizing the way in your daily actions.

Dakini   A powerful female deity associated with Tantric traditions. She has the power of flight and was almost certainly borrowed from pre-Aryan folklore. (*See also* TANTRA)

Dalai Lama   The head of Tibetan Buddhism and the spiritual and temporal leader of the Tibetan people. As the head of the Yellow Hat monks, he is regarded as the reincarnation of the BODHISATTVA Chenresi. The reincarnation of the deceased Dalai Lama is chosen by recognizing and selecting him in childhood. The chosen child is then trained to occupy the position that he held in the past life. The present Dalai Lama resides in Dharamsala since the occupation of Tibet by China.

Dana   *Lit. generosity, liberal giving, a gift*. One of the six PARAMITAS, or perfections, whose constant practice over lifetimes leads to enlightenment. The second precept of good conduct advises against taking things which are not given as gifts. Thus BHIKKUS (monks) should only accept that which is offered to them as *dana* by the laity, who, in turn, have the opportunity to provide for the SANGHA through their offering. (*See also* PARAMI)

Darsanamarga   The Path of Insight, which according to the BHAVANAKRAMA is the early stage in the development of a BODHISATTVA, when the adherent achieves direct experiential, non-conceptual knowledge or vision of emptiness. At this point come a host of powers such as control over future rebirths and the ability to see the Buddhas and visit their realms. (*See also* ASAIKSAMARGA; PRAYOGAMARGA; SAMBHARAMARGA)

Dasabhumika Sutra   A section of the AVATAMSAKA SUTRA that describes the ten stages of the BODHISATTVA's path to becoming a Buddha. (*See also* BHUMI)

Dasacakraksitigarbha Sutra   A Central-Asian SUTRA that is important to the veneration of the BODHISATTVA KSITIGARBHA. It is in this *sutra* that it is stated that the *bodhisattva* is the saviour of all sentient beings in the period after SAKYAMUNI's death and MAITREYA's birth.

Dayaka   A lay Buddhist who provides material support, very often food, to the Sangha. Ideally all lay Buddhists should maintain the SANGHA.

dGe-lugs (T)   The school of thought in Tibetan Buddhism which holds to the doctrine of *rang stong* (self-empty) and asserts that there is inherent existence in both the unenlightened and the 'Mind' of the enlightened. The true nature of existence is emptiness and there is no absolute or ultimate reality. (*See also* ANATMAN; JO NANG; TATHA-GATAGHARBA)

Deva   DEVAS are regarded as superhuman spiritual beings or the shining ones and their realms are regarded as one of the six destinations into which it is possible to be reborn. In Buddhist cosmology the gods reside in a paradise of delights where every kind of pleasure and luxury is available. Their lives are very long but eventually they will die and re-enter the cycle of SAMSARA. Consequently, even the gods envy and respect the human practitioner of the DHAMMA.

Dhamma (P) / Dharma (S)   The term has a variety of meanings (right, law, truth, justice, doctrine) but is usually understood as the Buddha's teachings and their application. As such, Dhamma is a universal law or ultimate truth. When written without a capital 'D' it refers to 'phenomena' or 'things' that make up all the constituents of the conditioned realm or SAMSARA. (*See also* BUDDHA; DHAMMAKAYA; NIRVANA)

Dhamma-cakkhu (P) *Lit. the eye of Dhamma.* The experiential insight or understanding of the Buddha's teachings which is accompanied by a spiritual transition. It is also known as 'stream-entry'. The first person to experience this transition was Kondanna, one of the ascetics who listened to the first sermon of the Buddha. (*See also* DHAMMACHAKKA)

Dhammachakka (P) / Dharmachakra (S) *Lit. the wheel of Dhamma.* The term used to describe Buddha's teachings as setting in motion an era of spiritual influence that began with the first sermon on the Four Noble Truths delivered at Varanasi. The SUTRA of the first sermon is known as *Dhamma-cakka-pavattana* or 'setting in motion of the Dhamma wheel'. (*See also* BUDDHA; DHAMMA)

Dhammakaya (P) / Dharmakaya (S) *Lit. the body of the law.* In the Mahayana tradition the Buddha is perceived as the personification of the Truth. He is beyond all dualities and conception and one with the eternal DHAMMA. Consequently everyone shares in the Buddha nature or principle of Buddhahood found within. In the THERAVADA tradition Dhammakaya refers to the totality of the Buddha's teachings. (*See also* NIRMANAKAYA; SAMBHOGAKAYA)

Dhammapada (P) / Dharmapada (S) *Lit. the path or way of the Dhamma.* An important book in the second basket (SUTTA PITAKA) of the Pali Canon consisting of 423 verses which are attributed to the Buddha. (*See also* NIKAYA)

Dhammas (P) / Dharmas (S) The building blocks of reality described in the ABHIDHAMMA. In the THERAVADA tradition there are eighty-two constituents that make up reality. Eighty-one are conditional, whilst one (NIRVANA) is unconditioned. Conditioned *dhammas* rise and cease in a continuous cycle. The Theravada Adhidhamma divides the dharmas into the following categories: (i) twenty-eight physical constituents which include the four elements, earth, water, fire and air;

(ii) fifty-two mental constituents of which twenty-five are morally good, thirteen morally neutral, and fourteen morally bad; (iii) Consciousness. The *dhammas* should not be confused with DHAMMA, the doctrine of the Buddha. (*See also* DHARMASUNYATTA)

Dhammavicaya (P)   Conquest by piety as opposed to the use of force. The Buddhist ideal of *Dhammavicaya* is the kingdom of ASHOKA after his conversion.

Dhammavijaya (P)   The search for truth or the longing to end the suffering caused by existence in the endless wheel of SAMSARA. The Buddha's quest for enlightenment is the ideal of the search for truth. (*See also* DHAMMA)

Dhammavinaya (P)   A term used in early Buddhism to refer to the doctrine or discipline which provided the basis for the community's religious life. (*See also* DHAMMA; SANGHA)

Dharana   The beginning of meditation, which consists of fixing the mind on one single object or thought. (*See also* BHAVANA; CITTAKAGGATA; VIPASSANA)

Dharani   Long sequences of syllables from scriptural passages used in Tantric Buddhism as spells or incantations and believed to provide special powers to invoke a god or goddess, generate good KARMA or help fix the concentration of a meditator. (*See also* KAMMA; TANTRA)

Dharmachakra (S)   *See* DHAMMACHAKKA.

Dharmadhatu   The world as seen by the Buddha. Known as the DHARMA realm, the universe is perceived as an interconnected flow without any hard edges and consisting of emptiness. This is the ultimate vision of the meditator and is the true form of the Buddha. (*See also* TRIKAYA)

Dharmaguptaka Vinaya   The rule of conduct used by Chinese orders of monks along with the SARVASTIVADA VINAYA. (*See also* MULASARVASTIVADA; VINAYA)

Dharmakara The BODHISATTVA who promises to build a PURE LAND in which the DHAMMA can be practised without problems. He presides over this blissful world as the Buddha AMIDA where he is joined by those human beings who have been devoted to him. The schools of Buddhism which followed the tradition of devotion or faith in the Amida Buddha became known as 'Pure Land'. (*See also* JODO)

Dharmakaya (S) *See* DHAMMAKAYA.

Dharmapada (S) *See* DHAMMAPADA.

Dharmasunyatta The early Mahayanan doctrine of the emptiness of DHARMAS. The belief that the primary building blocks of existence lack reality in the same way as everyday life lacks reality. The idea is first put forward in the LOKANUVARTANA SUTRA. (*See also* SHUNYATTA)

Dhutanga A list of thirteen ascetic practices that in the THERAVADA tradition mark the limits for Buddhist monks who wish to pursue asceticism. The Buddha warned against such practices, but indicated that they were acceptable if performed to cultivate being content with very little. The practices include eating once a day, sleeping without lying down, and living in cemeteries.

Dhyana Although sometimes used as a generic term for meditation, its more specific meaning applies to advanced meditation where intense or ecstatic concentration is attained by the practitioner which leads to SAMADHI. (*See also* CH'AN; VIPASSANA)

Dipamkara Buddha The Theravadin belief that the Buddha embarked on his quest to become enlightened by making a vow at the feet of Dipamkara, the twenty-fourth preceding Buddha.

Ditthi One of the four ASAVAS that delude the mind and prevent progress on the path to enlightenment. *Ditthi* refers to erroneous views concerning the nature of existence. For example, the belief that the soul is eternal.

Dogen (1200–54). The founder of the SOTO division of ZEN who after visiting China to find the true expression of the Buddha's teachings, transferred the teaching of Ts'ao-tung CH'AN to Japan, where it became known as Soto Zen.

Dokusan (J) A term used in ZEN Buddhism for a formal private meeting with the Master in his teaching chamber.

Dosa *Lit. hatred, anger, ill-will.* One of the three fires that have to be extinguished in order to achieve enlightenment. (*See also* MOHA; RAGA)

Dukkha (P) / Duhka (S) *Lit. suffering, misery, pain.* The essence of the teaching of the Buddha that the nature of existence and the condition of all beings except for the enlightened is suffering, or more accurately dissatisfaction. The Buddha presented the essence of his teaching on DUKKHA when he taught the Four Noble Truths in his first sermon at Sarnath near VARANASI. The Eightfold Path practised by Buddhists is the vehicle to end the suffering caused by conditioned existence. (*See also* SAMMA; TANHA)

G

Gahapati   A term used in the canonical texts for a head of a household, often depicted as giving the Buddha material support. This may indicate something about the class of the early converts to Buddhist teaching.

Gandavyuha Sutra   The culmination of the AVATAMSAKA SUTRA that presents the world from the viewpoint of the Buddha or BODHISATTVA's inner experience. The world is seen as a continuum of consciousness, a place of miracles, magic and visions. (*See also* DASABHUMIKA SUTRA)

Ganinnanse   The ganinnanse were a kind of lay monk in Ceylon who only took the lower ordination but wore white. Although they lived in monasteries, they were not celibate and maintained property. In the period between the late sixteenth century and 1753 there were no monks in Ceylon and the Buddhism was maintained by the ganin-nanse.

Gatha   A hymn or set of verses composed by monks in a state of spiritual insight. There are thousands of such inspired compositions from around the various parts of the Buddhist world.

Gautama   *See* SIDDATTHA GOTTAMA.

Gedo Zen (J)   The second of five types of ZEN Buddhism taught in Japan and known as 'the outside way'. It implies that the school acknowledges or utilizes teachings derived from non-Buddhist sources, such as

25

Hindu yoga, Confucian practices or the contemplative teachings of Christianity.

Gompa (T)   The term used in Tibetan Buddhism to describe a monastery or a place of meditation.

Gottama (P)   *See* SIDDATTHA GOTTAMA.

Gyogi   An eighth-century Japanese priest who helped to found the HUA-YEN school of Buddhism through his missionary activity and as joint founder of the Todaiji monastery, which remains to this day the centre of the KEGON (Hua-Yen) school in Japan. (*See also* BODHISENA)

H

Haiku (J)   A Japanese verse form introduced in the seventeenth century by Basho. It consists of seventeen syllables arranged in three lines of five, seven and five syllables respectively. The content was much influenced by ZEN and attempts to capture the moment or eternal present.

Hinayana   A term used in the MAHAYANA tradition to indicate the doctrine of the THERAVADA tradition. It literally means 'Lesser Vehicle'. Originally there were eighteen schools but only the Theravada, which was strong in South India and Sri Lanka, survived and flourished, spreading eastwards into South-East Asia. The school is very strict and believes that it represents the purest form of the Buddha's teachings. It is certainly the earliest school of Buddhism still surviving today.

Hokkegenki (J)   An eleventh-century collection of miracle stories which advocates the power of faith in the LOTUS SUTRA and the benefits of copying, reciting and promoting its contents.

Honen Shonen   (1133–1212) An influential Japanese teacher who popularized Amidism or AMIDA Buddhism and who believed after many years of searching that only the repetition of the name of the Amida Buddha could provide release from suffering. A monk at the age of nine he went on to found the JODO sect or 'PURE LAND' school.

Hua-Yen   *Lit. flower garden.* The school based on the doctrines of the Mahayanan text, AVATAMSAKA SUTRA. The HUA-YEN developed as a fully-fledged system, which believed itself to be the pinnacle of the

Buddha's teaching, in China. It was founded by five patriarchs but Fa-tsangh (seventh century CE) was the great systemizer of the tradition. Hua-Yen focuses on visionary experience and magic rather than philosophical speculation and the patriarchs are known for their miracles and healing abilities. Like CH'AN, Hua-Yen believes in sudden awakening to the ever-present Buddha nature already existing within. Later the school was transferred to Japan where it is known as KEGON.

J

Jaramarana Old age and death. The final link in the causal chain of existence which arises from JATI or birth. The Buddha left his palace to search for enlightenment after experiencing the shock of seeing old age, sickness and death. (*See also* NIDANAS; SAMSARA; SIDDATTHA GOTTAMA)

Jataka *Lit. birth stories.* A collection of 550 stories which form part of the THERAVADA Canon of scripture. They consist of accounts of the previous lives of the Buddha and provide a heritage of both moral teaching and mythology.

Jati Birth and rebirth. The fate of all sentient beings caught in the cycle of SAMSARA. The Buddhist doctrine of rebirth differs from that of Hinduism, as there is no belief in an eternal ATMAN which reincarnates again and again in different bodies. It is KAMMA itself which drives the wheel. In the causal chain of existence, *jati* arises from BHAVA and leads to the final link of old age and death or JARAMARANA. (*See also* NIDANAS)

Jhana (P) *See* DHYANA.

Jiriki *Lit. 'self' or 'own power'.* Term used by PURE LAND sects to describe ZEN as the way of salvation using self-power or self-effort as opposed to TARIKI or salvation through the intervention of an outside agency. The Pure Land schools of Buddhism believe that this age is so corrupt that it is not possible to achieve enlightenment without the assistance of the AMIDA Buddha.

Jizo (J)   *See* KSITIGARBHA.

Jnanaprasthana   A text that forms the central part of the ABHIDHARMA PITAKA written by the arhat Katyayaniputra around 200 BCE.

Jnana-sambhara   An aspect of the accumulation of merit gathered by a BODHISATTVA to achieve enlightenment. It is the perfection of wisdom brought about by the practice of the sixth PARAMI. (*See also* PANNA)

Jodo Shu (J)   A Japanese sect of PURE LAND Buddhism which proclaims devotion to the Buddha of Infinite Light and Great Compassion. Founded by HONEN, the disciple of Bencho. It is marked by the belief in salvation through faith in the AMIDA Buddha. (*See also* TARIKI)

Jo Nang Pa (T)   A Tibetan school of Buddhism that teaches the *gzhan stong* (other-empty) view that there is an ultimate reality or absolute, an unchanging eternal reality inherent in all sentient beings as the Buddha nature. This non-dual consciousness shines within all beings, both enlightened and unenlightened. (*See also* ANNATA; DGE-LUGS; TATHAGATAGHARBA)

Kahalinkarahara *Lit. material food or sustenance.* One of the four AHARAS or conditions which enable a sentient being to exist. (*See also* MANOSANCETANAHARA; PASSAHARA; VINNANAHARA)

Kaidan (J) A NICHIREN Buddhist place of worship and veneration, used to describe a building or an inner space.

Kalachakra A form of public initiation of empowerment given by the DALAI LAMA at BODH-GAYA and in the West. Thousands have attended the initiation as a way of receiving a blessing.

Kalama Sutta Sutra A SUTRA that has become popular in Western Buddhism as it appears to preach a message of individualism. It recounts a sermon of the Buddha in which he says that everyone should make up their own mind concerning religious truths and refer them to the touchstone of personal experience.

Kama Sensual pleasure or desire, especially sexual, which is regarded as the main obstacle to spiritual progress. It is one of the four ASAVAS or mental defilements and the elimination of KAMA is essential to achieve liberation from rebirth.

Kamadhatu In Buddhist cosmology there are three interlocking layers of existence that make up our world-system. *Kamadhatu* is the plane of existence for beings immersed in material desire or passion. DEVAS and humans are the inhabitants of this plane. (*See also* ARUPADHATU; RUPADHATU)

Kamma (P) / Karma (S)   Intentional actions in this and future lives performed by body, speech or mind that create a reaction of suffering or pleasure which affects one's circumstances in equal measure to the action. The Buddha's insistence that the effect depends on volition defines the distinction between Buddhist and Hindu understanding of *karma*. It is *kamma* which drives the wheel of SAMSARA rather than an omniscient creator deity. (*See also* JATI)

Kamma-phala / Kamma-vipaka   The fruit or result of an action which creates KARMA. (*See also* KAMMA; KUSALA)

Kapilavastu   The capital of the Sakya kingdom where the Buddha passed his childhood as a prince. It is near LUMBINI, the birthplace of the Buddha. (*See also* SIDDATTHA GOTTAMA)

Kappiya-karaka   A monastery attendant who is permitted to receive gifts, such as money, on behalf of a monk, which the latter are not normally allowed to accept.

Karandavyuha Sutra   An Indian SUTRA popular in Tibet which is devoted to praise of the BODHISATTVA AVALOKITESHWARA. It describes him as having one thousand arms and eleven heads and as creating the world and the Hindu gods. The *bodhisattva*'s harrowing of hell is also recounted.

Karma Pa (T)   The Tibetan lineage traced back to MARPA and MILAREPA, later divided into Black Hats and Red Hats. It is responsible for introducing the well-known Tibetan and Mongolian practice of lineage-tracing through reincarnation, used in the appointment of Dalai Lamas. (*See also* DALAI LAMA)

Karuna   *Lit. compassion*. Along with wisdom, compassion is essential for the human being who hopes to attain enlightenment and it is one of the two pillars of MAHAYANA Buddhism. Compassion is required for all beings that are suffering or caught in the wheel of SAMSARA and consists of love, charity, kindness and tolerance. (*See also* BODHISATTVA; BRAHMA VIHARA; PANNA).

Karunapundarika Sutra   A SUTRA which appears to have been written to counter the popularity of non-historic Buddhas. It argues that historic Buddhas such as SAKYAMUNI are superior in that they chose to teach in imperfect environments such as the world, whereas the legendary Buddhas choose to locate themselves in PURE LAND Buddha realms.

Kathavatthu   A text composed by the monk Tissa Moggaliputta at the bequest of Asoka during the Third Council. It became the final book of the ABHIDHAMMA PITAKA, and an affirmation of THERAVADA orthodoxy.

Kathina   A festival celebrated in all Theravadin Buddhist nations, after the rainy season, where the laity offer new robes to the monks. Usually material is provided which is cut up and sewn into a robe by the monks and offered to one of their number. The festival is named after the term applied to the robe.

Katikavata   A royal edict issued concerning changes to the rules of a monastic community. These are considered to be binding and have the same force as VINAYA regulations.

Kaya   The body or the material component of human beings and other living creatures. It can also be used to describe the 'body of the Law'. (*See also* DHAMMAKAYA)

Kegon (J)   The Japanese version of the HUA-YEN School developed by Ryonin (1072–1132). It was first introduced by Chinese missionaries and the Indian Bodhisena. Its natonal centre is the Todaiji monastery. (*See also* AVATAMSAKA; BODHISENA; GYOGI)

Kesa (J)   The robe worn over the shoulder by a monk, nun or priest in the ZEN school. (*See also* KOROMO)

Khandha   The five elements or aggregates that make up human nature (form, feeling, perception, mental formation and consciousness). As they are aggregates and will eventually dissolve into their constituent parts, they cause suffering when creatures cling to them as reality. (*See also* SKANDA)

Khandhaka   The portion of the VINAYA PITAKA that deals with the rules of community life. (*See also* SUTTA-VIBHANGA)

Khanti   *Lit. patience or forbearance.* One of the ten *paramitas* and an important virtue to be cultivated as one follows the DHAMMA. There is a story stating that Buddha described patience as the most important virtue for the BHIKKU to achieve as patience was required to wait for all the other fruits of the *Dhamma* to arrive. (*See also* PARAMI)

Kilesa (P) / Klesa (S)   Mental defilement such as greed, hatred or ignorance which must be eliminated by following the discipline of the Noble Eightfold Path in order to attain enlightenment. (*See also* BODHI)

Koan (J)   Used in RINZAI ZEN as a technique to create sudden awakening or develop intuition. A master will give the disciple a problem or riddle which cannot be solved by the intellect. When the intellect is short-circuited awakening can take place. The most famous Koan is the question 'What is the sound of one hand clapping?' (*See also* KUNG-AN)

Koromo (J)   The black or dark blue robe worn by a Japanese monk or priest. (*See also* KESA)

Ksitigarbha   A popular BODHISATTVA in China and Japan, where he is known as Jizo, who is believed to have been given the role of saving sentient beings between the period of SAKYAMUNI's death and MAITREYA's birth. Ksitigarbha is particularly associated with ancestors. His temples are used to offer prayers to them and he can be called upon to save deceased family members from entering hell realms or to rescue them from being hungry ghosts. In Japan he is also associated with the care of children and pregnant women. Small images of Jizo may be offered when a miscarriage or abortion takes place for the protection of the child. It is also believed that the bodhisattva enters the hell worlds and guides the beings contained there to higher realms. He is usually depicted as a monk carrying a staff with which he opens the doors of hell. (*See also* DASACAKRAKSITIGARBHA SUTRA; TI-TSANG PEN-YING CHING)

Kung-an (Ch)   In the CH'AN school, the *kung-an* is a dialogue between an awakened master and a disciple which leads to the disciple's sudden awakening. The dialogues usually consist of paradoxes that prevent reliance on the intellect. When CH'AN was introduced into Japan as ZEN, the *kung-an* was adapted into the koan of the RINZAI school. (*See also* KOAN)

Kusala   Good KAMMA which produces good effects and leads to more happiness or a better rebirth; that which is profitable or good.

Kwannon (J) / Kuan Yin (Ch)   The feminine aspect of the BODHISATTVA AVALOKITESHWARA, known as the Bodhisattva of Great Mercy. She is represented by a female figure sometimes with a child or seated on the back of a Chinese lion. In other forms she holds a lotus flower or is depicted carrying a vase containing the water of immortality. She is revered throughout China and Japan, and a fifty-metre-high statue of her outside Tokyo functions as a war memorial.

Laksana The generic term for the three conditions that bind all beings in SAMSARA. They are ANITYA, DUKKHA and ANATMAN or impermanence, suffering and devoid of essence. Understanding these three is seeing the world as it is and forms the Buddhist world-view.

Laukika The term used to describe the 'worldly' or 'unliberated' as opposed to *lokottara*, those that are beyond this world. (*See also* SAMSARA; NIRVANA)

Lin Ch'i A Chinese movement of CH'AN that emphasized the use of KUNG-AN and developed in Japan as RINZAI ZEN in the twelfth and thirteenth centuries.

Lokanuvartana Sutra An early SUTRA which includes the first appearance of doctrines concerning the supramundane Buddha. The Buddha is regarded as extraordinary, untainted by the world. His birth and death are both seen to be accompanied by miraculous events and he merely appears to perform the mundane activities of human life. (*See also* MAHASANGHITA)

Lokottaravada A sub-school of the MAHASANGHITA famous for its doctrines concerning the supramundame Buddha which were to enter into mainstream MAHAYANA thought. The idea of supramundanity asserts that the Buddha is omniscient, continuously in meditation and never asleep. His birth is miraculous and his everyday actions are illusory, mere appearances in order to conform to the customs of the world. (*See also* LOKANUVARTANA SUTRA)

Lotus Sutra   Properly known as SADDHARMAPUNDARIKA SUTRA, it is one of the earliest *sutras* and a major scripture in the MAHAYANA tradition. It describes the virtues of a BODHISATTVA, and emphasizes that all sentient beings can attain enlightenment. It was the basic text of the TI'EN T'AI School in China and is used by many new sects in Japanese forms of Buddhism.

Lumbini   The birthplace of SIDDATTHA GOTTAMA who became the Buddha. It is now situated in modern Nepal.

M

Madhyamaka   School of philosophy founded by NAGARJUNA, a South-Indian philosopher, in the second century BCE which asserted the middle position between realism and idealism. The School emphasized wisdom but gave little importance to DHYANA. Their aim was to annihilate the illusionary world through ruthless analysis. In particular they used analysis to counter-argue against belief in an absolute reality or independent existence. (*See also* PRASANGIKA; SVATANTRIKA)

Magadhi   The language spoken by the Sakyas, the community that the Buddha was born into. Magadha was one of the principal kingdoms of North India and was adjacent to the territory of the Sakyas. (*See also* SIDDATTHA GOTTAMA)

Magga (P) / Marga (S)   The Fourth Noble Truth which tells of the Path leading to the cessation of suffering which is known as the Middle Path or the Noble Eightfold Path. It is known as the Middle Path as it avoids the two extremes of asceticism and sense gratification, both tried by SIDDATTHA GOTTAMA before achieving Buddhahood. The Fourth Noble Truth provides the path for Buddhists to follow in order to find their way out of suffering. (*See also* CATTARI ARIYASACCANI; MAJJHIMA PATTIPADA; SAMMA)

Mahakasyapa   The monk who received enlightenment when observing the Buddha silently holding a flower. It is believed that his direct lineage of enlightened masters led to the founding of CH'AN and ZEN schools. (*See also* BODHIDHARMA)

Mahapadesha Sutra An ancient SUTRA which sets the method for establishing what is to count as an authentic text. It advocates relying on the existing corpus of authentic literature for coherence when assessing the new text. According to the *sutra*, personal authority is not to be taken into account.

Mahapari-nibbanasutta (P) A part of the PALI CANON that provides biographical details of the Buddha's life. It is an account of the last few months of his life and the details of his passing.

Mahaparinirvana Sutra (S) The MAHAYANA SUTRA which is also an account of the death and the final events of the Buddha's life. It is noteworthy as it teaches that the doctrine of ANATMAN was adopted by the Buddha to help destroy the lower ego self not to oppose the existence of the ATTA or eternal higher Self. The *sutra* is unique in that it teaches that the TATHAGATAGHARBA (the Buddha nature) is identical to the *atman*, the eternal self as taught in Hindu traditions. The *sutra* is also significant for its teaching that enlightenment and Buddhahood are the eventual goal of all sentient beings, even those who are perceived to be evil and beyond redemption.

Mahasanghita *Lit. the great Sangha.* Those who seceded from the orthodox Sthaviras at the Second Council held at Vesali about one hundred years after the PARINIBBANA of the Buddha. They insisted that monastic rules should be made easier but they also differed philosophically in that they set the standards required by an ARHANT at a lower level. They also played down the idea of the Buddha's humanity and saw him as some kind of manifestation of an eternal principle. (*See also* LOKANUVARTANA SUTRA; STHAVIRA)

Mahasthamaprapta A BODHISATTVA often depicted to the right of AMIDA in PURE LAND Buddhist traditions and used in visualizations.

Mahayana *Lit. the great vehicle.* It is prominent in Tibet, parts of Asia and the Far East. The Mahayana tradition emphasized the BODHISATTVA ideal and compassion was elevated alongside wisdom as the foremost virtue. Buddhahood was perceived as a transcendental principle which has existed over aeons. Individual Buddhas have therefore manifested in countless forms in countless places. Consequently the emphasis moves away from the historical Buddha. Finally, Mahayana Buddhism provided a new role for the laity either through devotional cults or the ideal of the enlightened householder. The earliest use of the term 'Mahayana' is found in India around the sixth century CE, however, the indications of Mahayana doctrines being held by independent groups of monks and laity can be found as far back as the first century BCE. It would appear that the idea of a separate Buddhist identity took centuries to develop, but the doctrines that came to be distinguished as Mahayana already existed in a variety of sacred texts and sutras.

Mahavairocana   *See* VAIROCANA.

Mahavamsa   *Lit. the great chronicle.* An important THERAVADA text written in Pali verse by the monk Mahanama in the sixth century and added to in the thirteenth and eighteenth centuries. The text chronicles the history of Sri Lankan Buddhism but also functions as an important signifier of Sinhalese nationalism, linking religion and nation.

Maitreya (S) / Metteya (P)   The name of the Buddha who is still to come and who has the nature of loving-kindness. He is the only BODHISATTVA acknowledged by the Theravadin School as well as the MAHAYANA. He will only be reborn in the human world when the DHAMMA established by SIDDHATTHA GOTTAMA is finished or worn out. The idea of a future Buddha has given rise to a number of messianic movments in China and Japan. Until his birth Maitreya lives in the heavenly realm known as TUSITA. This is believed to be very close to this world and consequently the future Buddha is already able to make visitations here. (*See also* BUDDHA)

Maitreyavyakarana Sutra   A Sanskrit SUTRA known as the *Prophecy of Maitreya* which contains the legend of the future Buddha and may have had a considerable influence on the development of his cult in MAHAYANA Buddhism. (*See also* MAITREYA)

Maitri (S) / Metta (P)   One of the BRAHMA VIHARAS or four sublime states cultivated by the Buddhist practitioner. It is also one of the ten perfections of the BODHISATTVA. *Metta* refers to loving-kindness or warm-hearted concern for the well-being of others. It is a love that should be extended outwards through meditation until it embraces everything equally. (*See also* BHAVANA)

Majjhima Patipada   The Middle Path taught by the Buddha as the way that leads to the end of suffering. It is known as the Middle Path because it avoids the two extremes of the pursuit of happiness through sense pleasure or ascetic practices. Both of these were experienced by the Buddha and rejected as leading to suffering. The Middle Path is laid out and developed as the Noble Eightfold Path which outlines the way that Buddhists should conduct their daily lives. (*See also* ARIYATTHANGIKAMAGGA; MAGGA; SAMMA)

Mala   String of 108 beads used in Buddhist practices in order to remember the repetition of sacred formulas. It has a similar function to a rosary.

Manas   The sense which co-ordinates the perceptions of the other five senses to provide a complete representation of the object perceived. The *manas* corresponds to the mind, in that it is a sense which conceives as ideas and thoughts the experiences or objects perceived by the sense organs.

Manjushri   A celestial Tibetan BODHISATTVA of the tenth stage, where Buddhahood is achieved. Manjushri is equal in status to AVALOKITESVARA, the *bodhisattva* of compassion. Manjushri who is represented as a youth, is considered to be the repository of wisdom, and thus the two *bodhisattvas* manifest the two principles of MAHAYANA Buddhism. The cult of Manjushri has come to the West and is practised by the New Kadampa Tradition. Often his level of realization is considered to be so high that he is regarded as a Buddha with his own Buddha realm. (*See also* KARUNA; PANNA)

Manjushrinamasangiti   An important Tantric text used in Tibet for chanting and which maintains the supremacy of MANJUSHRI. The text states that Manjushri is the enlightener of all the Buddhas. (*See also* TANTRA)

Manosancetanahara One of the four AHARAS or conditions that nourish the clinging to existence that manifests itself in all living creatures except for the enlightened. It refers to mental volition or self-will. (*See also* KAHALINKARAHARA; PASSAHARA; VINNANAHARA)

Mantra A sacred formula or chant usually in Sanskrit which can be recited verbally or visualized. The essence of a Tantric deity is contained in its MANTRA. The repetition of *mantras* can bring magical powers, prevent idle chatter and protect the mind by providing an everyday spiritual connection. The most famous Buddhist *mantra* is OM MANE PADME HUM used by Tibetan Buddhists. (*See also* TANTRA)

Mappo (J) The Japanese Buddhist belief in ages of spiritual decline or the final days of the DHAMMA, often used in the doctrines of new Buddhist sects who teach revival or rejuvenation of the *Dhamma*. Very often, such movements draw upon the LOTUS SUTRA as their definitive text.

Mara *Lit. death*. The Evil One or the Tempter who tried to prevent the Buddha achieving enlightenment when sitting under the BODHI TREE. In Buddhist mythology, his role is to maintain delusion and desire in order to keep beings enchained to the wheel of SAMSARA. (*See also* BODHI; SIDDATTHA GOTTAMA)

Marga *See* MAGGA.

Marpa (1012–96) The famous wealthy Tibetan layman and translator who travelled in India and received instruction from the sage Naropa. On return to Tibet, he became the master of the better-known MILAREPA, the great Tibetan yogi and poet. Marpa, Milarepa and his disciple Gampopa were responsible for founding the Kaagyu Order, better known as the Red Hats.

Maya The mother of the Buddha, who according to legend dreamed that a white elephant had entered her body through the right side when she conceived. She gave birth to the Buddha in the wooded garden of LUMBINI, near Kapilavastu. (*See also* SIDDATTHA GOTTAMA)

Maya *Lit. illusion.* The reality of everyday perception which is regarded as an illusionary or limiting mode of experience of the complex and multi-faceted universe. (*See also* SAMSARA)

Megha The forerunner of the BODHISATTVA ideal believed in by MAHAYANA Buddhists. Megha was an ascetic who met with the previous Buddha, Dipamkara. If Megha had chosen to become an enlightened ARHANT, there would have been no SIDDATTHA GOTTAMA. Instead, Megha chose to follow the ten *paramitas*, or path to perfection and entered the way of the *bodhisattva*. After many lifetimes he was reborn as Siddattha Gottama. (*See also* PARAMI)

Metta *See* MAITRI.

Metta Sutta A scripture that is one of the most widely used in the PALI CANON and which describes the Nature of loving-kindness. (*See also* MAITRI)

Metteya (P) *See* MAITREYA.

Miccha That which is false or untrue. It usually refers to wrong views or wrong opinions that derive from an illusionary or limited understanding of the nature of reality. (*See also* MAYA; SAMSARA)

Milarepa (1040–1123) A disciple of MARPA who had previously been a magician. He was treated with great harshness by his master and subjected to numerous tests to expiate his bad *karma*. After six years he was initiated and passed the remainder of his life as a wandering yogi living in caves in the Himalayas. Milarepa wrote many poems and attracted a large number of disciples. He is a beloved figure of Tibetan Buddhism.

Milendra The Greek king, Menandros, who ruled over a kingdom in Bactria, now in modern Afghanistan. He was attracted to Buddhism and his discussions concerning his spiritual conflict are recorded in question and answer form with a monk named Nagasena. They are known as the *Milinda-Panha*, an important Pali text that is not part of the Canon. The main discussion revolves around the problem of how the Buddha could have believed in rebirth without acknowledging an incarnating permanent self.

Moggallana   One of the prominent disciples of the Buddha who is regarded as a master of meditation and psychic powers.

Moha   *Lit. delusion*, *stupidity*, *dullness*. One of the three fires that have to be extinguished in order to provide the equanimity that is necessary in order to attain enlightenment. (*See also* DOSA; RAGA)

Mosadhamma (P)   The expression used by the Buddha to describe unreality or the belief in the permanence of phenomena. (*See also* MAYA; NIRVANA; SAMSARA)

Mudda (P) / Mudra (S)   *Lit. A seal or a symbol*. Ritual hand gestures which have deep symbolic significance and association with blessings usually related to a particular Tantric deity. (*See also* TANTRA)

Mudita   One of the four sublime states or BRAHMA VIHARAS experienced by an advanced practitioner. *Mudita* is sympathetic joy or the experience of sharing the success and achievements of others without feelings of hostility or competitive envy at their success. (*See also* KARUNA; METTA; UPEKKHA)

Mularsarvastivada   The non-Mahayana monastic code which was imposed on Tibetan monks by the king Khri Ide gtsugn brtan in the ninth century and translated into Tibetan. (*See also* DHARMAGUPTAKA VINAYA; SARVASTIVADA; VINAYA)

N

Nagarjuna   Teacher who founded the MADHYAMAKA School of philosophy in the second century BCE. He was born in Maharashtra, but after becoming a monk lived in Andhra. He was a prolific writer who systemized the *Perfection of Wisdom* SUTRA which formed the basis of the Madhyamaka School. The most radical assertion made by Nagarjuna, based on the *Perfection of Wisdom* SUTRA, was that all things are empty or had no existence independent of external circumstances. Very little is known about his life, and most accounts are hagiographic. He is sometimes known as the second Buddha and his writings form the basis of the Madhyamaka literature. They are the analytical works: *Madhyamakakarika, Yuktisastika, Sunyatasaptati, Vigrahavyvartani, Vaidalyaprakarana* and the lost *Vyavaharasiddhi*. In addition there are collections of hymns and shorter treatises and epistles.

Nagas (S)   Mythical serpents which protect Buddhas and Buddhists. In Indian mythology the *Nagas* are symbols of the initiates into wisdom.

Nairmanikakaya   Manifestation bodies of the Buddha which refer to the belief that the Buddha can manifest as anything, animal or human, Buddhist or non-Buddhist, for the specific benefit of another, usually to teach a specific point through skilful means. (*See also* BUDDHAKAYA)

Nama   *Lit. name.* Used collectively for the aspects of the mind or four of the five *Khandhas* leaving out form or *rupa*. (*See also* SKANDA; VEDANA; VINNANA).

Nama Rupa *Lit. name and form.* Used as a collective term for all the five KHANDAS. In the context of the *Khandhas*, it refers to mind and body but it can also be used as a description of all phenomenal existence. It is also a part of the causal chain of existence arising out of *vinnana* and leading to *salayatana*. (*See also* NAMA; NIDANAS; RUPA; SALAYATANA; SAMSARA; VINNANA)

Nembutsu (J) The Japanese translation of the Chinese NIEN-FO. It describes the practice of chanting the name of AMIDA Buddha that is central to PURE LAND schools of Buddhism. The great practitioner of Japanese Pure Land is HONEN who is believed to have practised the Nembutsu 70,000 times a day.

Neyartha (P) / Nitartha (S) The distinction made between texts that require interpretion and those which are taken literally. It forms the basis of Buddhist hermeneutics.

Nibbana (P) / Nirvana (S) The indescribable state of ultimate peace or bliss achieved by the enlightened and the supreme goal of all sentient beings. It indicates the blowing out or extinction of the self and the annihilation of all *karma*. It is the only way to end the continuous cycle of birth and rebirth on the wheel of SAMSARA. However, in MAHAYANA Buddhism there are several types of Nirvana, from the Nirvana of the ARHANT and the PRATYEKABUDDHA which are rejected as final goals, to the full Nirvana of the Buddha. (*See also* BODHISATTVA; BUDDHA; KAMMA)

Nichiren (J) (b. 1222). A Japanese monk, skilled in oratory and textual study, who believed that Buddhism was lost in an age of decline (MAPPO). Thus the Buddha protectors of Japan have left the country to its fate. He criticizes contemporary Buddhist sects in Japan, such as ZEN or AMIDA, as deviations and advocates that the nation should return to the veneration of SAKYAMUNI as described in the LOTUS SUTRA. Until such time disasters will fall upon the people. Only the Lotus Sutra is true and all that the people need to do in the age of Mappo is have faith in its contents. From Japan this true message will spread to the world. (*See also* NICHIREN SHOSHU; NIHONZAN MYOHONJI; SOKA GAKKAI; RISSHO KOSEI KAI)

Nichiren Shoshu (J)   A number of Japanese Buddhist sects, based on the teachings of NICHIREN, and believing Nichiren to be the Buddha of the MAPPO age. Thus Nichiren is perceived to be the cosmic Buddha identified with SAKYAMUNI in the LOTUS SUTRA. Nichiren shoshu is distinguished by its staunch advocacy of the Lotus Sutra as the sole repository of truth in the current age of DHAMMA decline, the chanting of *namu myo, ho renge kyo*, often to the beat of a drum, and reverence of a MANDALA centred on Sakyamuni and designed by Nichiren. All the movements advocate worldly success, active prosyletization which brings social benefits, therapy, and the avoidance of monasticism to concentrate on the lay elements of MAHAYANA Buddhism. (*See also* NIHONZAN MYOHONJI; RISSHO KOSEI KAI; SOKA GAKKAI)

Nidanas (P)   The causal chain which describes the way in which being or individual existence takes place. Each *nidana* or link is mutually dependent on the other and expresses the process taught by the Buddha 'that arising, this becomes; this ceasing to be, that ceases to be'. Therefore, all things arise and exist due to the presence of something else, and cease to exist once these conditions are removed. The twelve *nidanas* are the links in the chain. The root cause is ignorance, which gives rise to constructing activities, followed by consciousness, mind and body, the six senses, sensory stimulation, feeling, craving, grasping, existence, birth, ageing and death. (*See also* AVIDYA; BHAVA; JARAMARANA; JATI; NAMA-RUPA; PATICCA-SAMUPPADA; PHASSA; SALAYATANA; SANKHARA; TANHA; UPADANA; VEDANA; VINNANA)

Nien-fo (Ch)   The recitation of the AMIDA Buddha's name as a loving expression of receiving his grace to enter the PURE LAND or celestial realm where the Buddha teaches. (*See also* NEMBUTSU)

Nihonzan Myohonji   A NICHIREN-inspired movement founded in the early twentieth century in Japan. It is very nationalistic and similar to other Nichiren movements in seeing Japan as the base for converting the world. The founder, Nichidatsu Fuji, was a pacifist and part of his campaign to promote world peace consisted of constructing stupas or 'peace pagodas' throughout the world. Two exist in Britain, one in Milton Keynes and the other in Battersea Park, London. (*See also* NICHIREN SHOSHU)

Nikaya   A *nikaya* refers to a group of THERAVADA monks who observe their own ordination ceremonies, or who have variations on the PATTIMOKKHA or precepts, to the degree that they can be defined as a sub-sect within the wider community. When written with a capital letter, *Nikaya* refers to a collection of five sets of discourses and texts that form the SUTTA PITAKA, the second of the three baskets of scripture that make up the PALI CANON. They are *Digha Nikaya*, *Majjhima Nikaya*, *Samyutta Nikaya*, *Anguttara Nikaya* and *Khuddaka Nikaya*.

Nirmanakaya (S)   *Lit. transformation or appearance body.* One of the three bodies of the Buddha according to MAHAYANA doctrine. The *Nirmanakaya* refers to the physical body which the Buddha uses to appear in the world in order to help suffering beings. It also applies to apparitions or visions of the Buddha that may occur in dreams. (*See also* DHAMMAKAYA; SAMBHOGAKAYA; TRIPIKAYA)

Nirodha   The third of the Four Noble Truths taught by the Buddha which refers to extinction or cessation of desire and brings to an end all suffering. It will also bring to end all finite existence as experienced on the wheel of SAMSARA. It therefore equates with NIRVANA as the ultimate goal of Buddhism and is attainable through the Noble Eightfold Path. (*See also* CATTORI ARIYASACCANI)

Nirvana   *See* NIBBANA.

Nirvana Sutra   A partisan MAHAYANA text written around 200–400 CE which is critical of the THERAVADA school and claims that Buddha gave a secret teaching before his death. The SUTRA claims that anyone insulting the Mahayana tradition is destined for extreme punishment.

Nissaya   The four 'resorts' of a monk which are part of the instructions on ordination. They are: eating food obtained by begging; wearing rags taken from a rubbish heap; living underneath trees; and using fermented cattle urine as medicine. The Buddha never taught such asceticism but for a wandering monk they remain as the bottom line of subsistence.

Om mane padme hum (T) The most famous MANTRA used in Tibetan Tantric Buddhism. Literally it means 'Hail to the Jewel in the Lotus' and its popularity in Tibet is indisputable. All classes of Buddhists recite it, inscribe it on flags, paint it on walls and enclose it in turning prayer-wheels. It functions as a symbolic and condensed expression of the path to enlightenment. (*See also* TANTRA)

P

Pabbaja (P) / Pravrajya (S) *Lit. going forth.* Renunciation of the world. It is the admission of the desire to become a monk made to the SANGHA undertaken before formal training begins. The novice monk is accepted by a single interviewer in the presence of his family. He is shaved, given his robes and repeats the Three Refuges. (*See also* BHIKKU; SAMANERA; UPASAMPADA)

Paccaya The essential requirements of a monk's life that should only be received as gifts given by the laity. (*See also* DANA)

Padmasambhava An eighth-century Indian yogi who embodies the Tantric ideal of the wandering magician free from all external constraints. It is believed that after the first monastery was founded in Tibet, Tibetan local demons hindered the development of Buddhism. Padmasambhava was invited to Tibet to defeat the demons with his siddha power. Since the fourteenth century he has been revered as a Buddha with even more power than Sakyamuni.

Padmasana The Lotus position commonly used for meditation. It is a cross-legged position where both ankles are placed on the thigh of the opposite leg.

Pali The scriptural and liturgical language of THERAVADA Buddhism. Although now a dead language, it is one of the most important languages for the preservation of the DHAMMA. It was introduced in

Sri Lanka by Theravadins for the formal writing down of the DHAMMA in the first century BCE. (*See also* PALI CANON)

Pali Canon   The formal canon of scripture for the Theravadin Buddhists compiled in Sri Lanka at the Fourth Council held at the Aloka Cave. It is divided into three *pitakas* or 'baskets' known as VINAYA, SUTTA, ABHIDHARMA. (*See also* PITAKA; TIPITAKA)

Pamsu-kulika   An ascetic community of monks who came into prominence around 700 CE and dressed in rags.

Pancasila   The five rules or precepts binding on all Buddhists. They are: avoidance of killing or even sanctioning the destruction of a living being; abstention from taking anything which is not given; avoidance of unlawful sexual intercourse; abstention from falsehood; and finally abstention from alcohol or other intoxicants.

Pancavimsati Sutra   A part of the PRAJNAPRAMITRA literature that teaches the doctrine that *bodhisattvas* renounce even Buddhahood until all beings have been enlightened. However, the text makes little or no differentiation between the powers of a Buddha and that of a *bodhisattva*.

Panchen Lama (T)   The second highest rank after the DALAI LAMA in the Gelugpa School of Tibetan Buddhism. As with the Dalai Lama, on the death of the incumbent, the new Panchen Lama is searched for in the body of a small child. He is believed to be the manifestation of AMIDA Buddha.

Panna (P) / Prajna (S)   Wisdom or discernment. It refers to understanding the true Nature of things which leads to the freedom from bondage to SAMSARA and eventual NIRVANA. Wisdom and meditation (DHYANA) are the two highest virtues of Buddhism and the mainstays of the DHAMMA. The state of *prajna* or wisdom exists outside time and duality and the cultivation of wisdom is one of the six *paramitas* which according to MAHAYANA tradition lead to the state of BODHISATTVA. Wisdom and compassion are the two pillars of the Mahayana tradition. (*See also* PARAMI; MANJUSHRI)

Parajika   *Lit. entailing defeat.* The four offences that can incur the punishment of expulsion from monastic life. They are: sexual intercourse; taking something not given; intentionally causing loss of life to a human being; and falsely claiming miraculous powers. Nuns have four more which are: touching a man between his shoulders and his knees; allowing men physical contact; concealing another nun's offence; and taking the side of a suspended monk. (*See also* PATIMOKKHA; SANGHA)

Paramartha-satya   The ultimate truth. Some MAHAYANA Buddhists, for example, regard the Buddha nature as the ultimate form of the truth. NAGARJUNA, the founder of the Madhyamaka school, declared that on the level of *Paramartha-satya*, the conventional world did not exist, and it is only on the plain of the conditioned world that the teachings of the Buddha exist.

Parami (P) / Paramita (S)   A perfection or virtue. One of the attainments necessary for Buddhahood. It consists of the highest possible development of DANA, SILA, KSHANTI, VIRIYA, DHYANA and PANNA. These are regarded as the six stages of spiritual perfection required by a Bodhisattva on the journey to Buddhahood.

Parinibbana (P) / Parinirvana (S)   Final and complete NIRVANA achieved on the death of a Buddha after which there is no more rebirth.

Parisad   The four categories of Buddhists which make up the complete community. It is comprised of the Order of the SANGHA (monks, nuns) and male and female laity. (*See also* BHIKKU; BHIKKUNI)

Pasada   A term commonly used in the Pali canon to signify faith. It differs from SHRADDHA, which carries a more intellectual understanding of faith arising from rational reflection on doctrine. *Pasada* is more concerned with the emotional well-being that comes from feeling that something is true.

Passahara   One of the four AHARAS or nourishments which feed the condition that keeps a being in the wheel of SAMSARA. *Passahara* refers to the contact of the sense organs with the external world.

Paticca-samuppada (P) / Pratitya-samutpada (S)   The Chain of Dependent Causation. The causal sequence of the wheel of life, or twelve distinct links in the chain of causation which are all interdependent. As the wheel of life is a cycle, there is no primal cause, although it is recognized that ignorance is the first link in the chain. The Buddha taught that failure to understand the nature of the Chain of Dependent Causation resulted in the deep, almost impenetrable, entanglement in SAMSARA. In some descriptions it is the knowledge of the Chain of Causation that marked the Buddha's enlightenment. (*See also* NIDANAS)

Patimokkha (P) / Pratimoksha (S)   The code of monastic rules contained in the VINAYA PITAKA which are binding on all members of the SANGHA. They are traditionally chanted by monastic communities at each full moon. While there are 227 variant versions in the THERAVADA tradition, the differences only apply to the minor rules concerning etiquette. The PATIMOKKHA ceremony, where all the assembled monks repeat the 227 precepts, is repeated every fortnight. After each category of offence all the monks are asked by their preceptor if they are pure. (*See also* UPOSATHA)

Peta (P) / Preta (S)   *Lit. the hungry ghosts.* One of the six types of being that inhabit the three realms in Buddhist cosmology. They are the shades of the dead or disembodied spirits who inhabit the realms of hell. They are still within the realm of KAMADHATU, the realm of desire, and it is traditional in some forms of MAHAYANA Buddhism to give them some of the offerings provided at *puja*. They are often depicted with bloated stomachs and tiny mouths, which represents their insatiable desires. After an interminable period of purgatory, they are released to continue on the wheel of SAMSARA. In Buddhism, a period in hell cannot last longer than the KAMMA, which brought it about.

Phassa   The sense of touch which is the strongest of the six sense organs. It is the sixth link in the chain of causation, dependent on SALAYATANA, and giving rise to VEDANA. (*See also* NIDANAS)

Pindapata   The alms round expected of the Buddhist monk, still the norm in South-East Asia where the monks file into the towns and villages and offer up their bowls to the laity for alms.

Pirit   A Sri Lankan charm or ceremony which protects from evil, used in popular or rural Buddhism.

Pitaka   *Lit. basket.* Used to refer to the three collections of scripture which make up the PALI CANON. (*See also* ABHIDHARMA; SUTTA; TIPITAKA; VINAYA)

Posan   Sri Lankan festival held on the full moon in June to celebrate the arrival of Buddhism, brought to the island by the Venerable Malinda.

Poya   A Sinhalese alternative name for UPOSATHA Days, also used by Western Buddhists.

Pradakshina Sutra   A SUTRA which advocates the veneration of *stupas*. (*See also* STUPA)

Prajna (S)   *See* PANNA.

Prajnaparamita   A body of Indian literature, particularly the *Astasahasrika* (the 8,000-verse *Perfection of Wisdom*) that is significant in the development of early Mahayanan ideas and doctrines. The earliest texts were written between 100 BCE and 100 CE. (*See also* MAHAYANA)

Pramanas   The logical intellectual endeavour to discover valid sources of knowledge to engage in philosophical debate with non-Buddhist opponents. It became a part of the standard syllabus in Buddhist universities.

Pranidhana   The vow to achieve Buddhahood which along with the six perfections (*paramitas*) is considered by some MAHAYANA schools to be an essential prerequisite to entering on the path followed by a BODHISATTVA. (*See also* PARAMI)

Prasangika   A sub-division of the MADHYAMAKA believed to have been founded by Buddhapalita (470–540). However, it was Candrakirti (600–50) who first argued in defence of Buddhapalita's position against his arch rival Bhavaviveka (500–70), the founder of the SVATANTRIKA sub-division. The dispute seemed to be one of methodology. The use of analytical argument to oppose doctrines of independent existence or the existence of an absolute were not undermined. The Prasangika asserted that such arguments should try to indicate the error of an opponent's ways by referring to the consequences for the person himself; while the Svatantrika posited that such arguments must follow the logical structure recognized by other Indian schools of thought. The two sub-divisions were to take on significance in Tibet where their arguments on methodology remain a significant part of Buddhist education.

Prasrabdhi   A refined state of purely mental spiritual happiness in which the practitioner is absorbed in bliss with little awareness of physical surroundings. It is one of the seven stages on the road to enlightenment. (*See also* PRITI; SAMADHI; SMRITI; UPEKKHA; VIRIYA)

Pratimoksha (S)   *See* PATIMOKKHA.

Pratitya-samutpada   *See* PATICCA-SAMUPPADA.

Pratyekabuddha   A term for an awakened human being who achieves enlightenment independently like the Buddha but who chooses not to teach. (*See also* ARHANT; BODHISATTVA; BUDDHA)

Pratyutpannabuddhasammukha-vasthitassamadhi Sutra   A SUTRA used by MAHAYANA traditions to support their doctrines concerning the significance of the Buddhist laity and their ability to attain the same levels of enlightenment as the monks. The *sutra* demonstrates this doctrinal position by recounting the incident of the Buddha delivering the *sutra* to an audience of both monks and *bodhisattvas*, but the key element of the audience was five hundred householder *bodhisattvas* to whom the *sutra* is addressed. It is said that the text would be lost and rediscovered during a period of decay of the *Dhamma*. The lay *bodhisattvas* request the Buddha to be reborn as the discoverer of the *sutra* in the future. (*See also* ASOKADATTAVYAKARANA SUTRA; BHADRAMAYAKARAVYAKARANA SUTRA; BODHISATTVA; MAHAYANA; VIMALAKAKIRTINIRDESA SUTRA)

Pratyutpanna Samadhi A meditation in which the practitioner enters one-pointed concentration through visualization of the Buddha. It is commonly practised in Chinese AMIDA traditions. The practitioner (monk or lay, male or female) first has to completely follow the moral code of a practising Buddhist. They then enter into a retreat and reflect upon the place where the Amida Buddha dwells. The Buddha is visualized as sitting upon a throne and teaching the DHARMA immediately in front of the practitioner. (*See also* BUDDHANUSMRITI)

Pravrajya (S) *See* PABBAJA.

Prayogamarga The Path of Preparation, which according to the BHAVANAKRAMA is the second stage in the development of a BODHISATTVA, when the adherent remains in the condition of being an ordinary person but is beginning to remove all conceptual awareness and duality in readiness for direct apprehension of emptiness. There is no longer rebirth in the lower realms and the *bodhisattva* attains deep faith, perseverance, powers of meditation and recollection of the DHARMA. (*See also* ASAIKSAMARGA; DARSANA-MARGA; SAMBHARAMARGA)

Preta (S) *See* PETA.

Priti A release of ecstatic energy which fills the practitioner with rapture. It is considered to be the fourth of the seven stages towards enlightenment. It follows from VIRIYA and leads on to PRASRABDHI once the experience has settled down and its emotional aspects have quietened. (*See also* SAMADHI; UPEKKHA)

Pudgalavadin (S) / Puggalavadin (P) *Lit. personalists.* The second group of Buddhists to break away from the STHAVIRAVADA. They challenged the doctrine of ANATTA by asserting that there was a very subtle transcendental Self only experienced by Buddhas. They claimed that this Self was ultimate reality and should not be confused with the false self-identification accurately diagnosed by the Buddha.

Punna kamma The purifying action that brings the virtuous Buddhist *karmic* rewards in this and future lives. To perform a good action is to purify one's state of mind. In meditation, purification takes place without any accompanying action. Thus the Buddha replaced the old Vedic or brahminical concept where right action was perceived to be ritually correct action. (*See also* KAMMA)

Pure Land *See* AMIDA.

Purvashaila A sub-sect of the MAHASANGHITA which taught that the DHAMMAS lack inherent existence. This doctrine was later associated with MAHAYANA traditions.

R

Ragas   *Lit. passion, greed or uncontrolled lust.* One of the three fires that have to be extinguished in order to achieve Enlightenment. (*See also* DOSA; MOHA)

Rahula   *Lit. fetter.* The son of SIDDATTHA GOTTAMA who was born shortly before his father set out to seek Enlightenment. He is believed to have entered the SANGHA at the age of fifteen.

Rang stong (T)   *Lit. self-empty.* The Tibetan doctrine that asserts that there is no absolute being and that even the DHAMMAKAYA is empty of essential existence. (*See also* TATHAGATAGHARBA; DGE-LUGS)

Ratnagotravibhaga   Also known as the *Uttaratantra*, this important text for Tibetan Buddhists is the source of information on the relationship between the DHAMMAKAYA, the TATHAGATAGHARBA and human consciousness.

Ratnasambhava   *Lit. the jewel-born one.* One of the five main celestial Buddhas, known as Dhyani Buddhas, venerated in Tibetan Tantric traditions. (*See also* TANTRA; YIDAM)

Rinzai (J)   A large sect of ZEN and the first school to arrive from China. It was introduced to Japan by the monk Eisai (1141–1215) and emphasized the use of KOAN in its teaching. The RINZAI School was adopted by the Samurai rulers and assisted in the spread of Chinese culture within the ruling classes of Japan.

Rissho Ankoku Ron (J)   Lit. *Essay on the Establishment of Righteousness and the Security of the Country.* An important Japanese text written by NICHIREN in the form of question and answers between a Visitor and the Master (Nichiren). The text presents most of the teachings of Nichiren in answer to the question 'Why is the world in such a terrible state?' (*See also* NICHIREN SHOSHU)

Rissho Kosei-Kai (J)   A Japanese religious movement that focuses upon the LOTUS SUTRA, founded in 1938 by Niwano Nikkyo (b.1906) and Nagamuna Myoko (1889–1957). The early emphasis was on faith healing by chanting from the Lotus Sutra. After 1957, the movement changed its emphasis from healing physical ailments to the discovery of the eternal Buddha as revealed in the Lotus Sutra. (*See also* NICHIREN; NICHIREN SHOSHU)

Ritsu (J)   A Japanese Buddhist sect begun in 754 CE by Ganjin and his followers who had arrived in Japan to perform the proper ceremonies for ordination into the SANGHA. The sect that developed was primarily concerned with carrying out the teachings of the VINAYA PITAKA, the code of discipline that governs the life of monks.

Rupa   *Lit. form.* As physical form it is the first of the five KHANDHAS but it is also used to describe the realm of form as opposed to the formless realms. (*See also* ARUPADHATU; NAMARUPA; RUPADHATU)

Rupadhatu / Rupaloka   The realm of form that is the middle one of the three layers that make up the world system in Buddhist cosmology. (*See also* ARUPADHATU; KAMADHATU)

S

Sacca (P) / Satya (S)   Used for both absolute and relative Truth, but it usually refers to the Four Noble Truths. (*See also* CATTARI ARIYASACCANI)

Sadaparibhuta   A BODHISATTVA, who according to the LOTUS SUTRA was abused for publicly teaching that all beings would eventually become Buddhas and were therefore worthy of reverence.

Saddha (S)   *Lit. confidence or faith. Saddha* is not faith in the sense of belief in the teachings of the Buddha. The Buddhist should ideally experience or understand rather than merely believe; consequently *saddha* is more correctly translated as confidence or conviction born out of experience rather than belief. However, many Buddhists do have an element of faith in the Three Jewels, that is in the Buddha, the DHAMMA and the SANGHA. (*See also* BUDDHA)

Saddharmapundarika Sutra (S)   *Lit. 'Sutra of the Lotus of the Good Law'.* An important MAHAYANA text commonly known as the LOTUS SUTRA. It was written in India in the second century CE in Sanskrit and claims to be the teaching of the transcendent Buddha who is depicted as exultant on a Himalayan mountaintop. It teaches the identification of the transcendent Buddha with the historical Buddha through proclaiming the doctrine that the Buddha's birth and life was a skilful device undertaken to teach the DHAMMA to humanity.

Sadhana   Spiritual practices or disciplines, usually meditations concerned with visualizations of Bodhisattvas, Buddhas and *mandalas*, all used in Tibetan Tantric traditions. (*See also* BODHISATTVA; YIDAM)

Sadhanamala   Tantric collections of *sadhanas* devoted to visualization exercises and including *mandalas*, many of which contain Buddhas and Bodhisattvas in the centre. (*See also* SADHANA; TANTRA)

Saha   The world sphere where human beings live and the Buddha field or sphere of influence of SAKYAMUNI, the place where he taught and passed through the various incarnations as a BODHISATTVA. It will remain under the influence of Sakyamuni until the birth of MAITREYA. (*See also* BUDDHAKSHETRA)

Saicho (J)   The founder of the Tendai school of Japanese Buddhism. As a young monk in 788 CE, he was dissatisfied with the corruption of his monastery and left to establish a new community strictly based upon the rules of the VINAYA PITAKA. He studied CH'AN, VINAYA and T'IEN-T'AI in China and on his return to Japan created a single system from all the elements, including Shinto, which became known as Tendai.

Saijojo (J)   The fifth and highest form of ZEN believed to be the culmination of all Buddhist Zen paths and the one practised by the Buddhas themselves.

Saiksya-dharmas   Part of the PATTIMOKKHA based on the VINAYA PITAKA regulations for monastic life which outline the minor rules concerning etiquette.

Sakrdagamin   *Lit. the once-returner.* A stage on the journey to enlightenment in which the practitioner will only have one more rebirth during which he/she will attain the goal of NIRVANA. (*See also* SAMYOJANA)

Sakyamuni (P) / Shakyamuni (S)   *Lit. the sage of the Sakyas* (the tribe of the Buddha). One of the titles given to the historical Buddha. (*See also* SIDDATTHA GOTTAMA)

Salayatana   The six organs of sense and their functions which are one of the NIDANAS in the chain of causation. The *Salayatanas* are dependent upon the NAMARUPA and the PHASSA is in turn dependent upon the *Salayatanas*.

Samadhi   The last stage of the Noble Eightfold Path before NIRVANA. It is used to describe intense concentration in meditation which leads to awareness of reality or a state of equanimity where the condition of duality caused by thought can no longer disturb the surface of the Ocean of Truth. In this state the distinctions between subject, object and their relationship are transcended. (*See also* DHYANA)

Samadhi Sutras   A collection of MAHAYANA SUTRAS that teach about meditation states. They include the *Surangama-samadhi sutra*, *Pratyutpanna Sutra* and the *Samadhiraja Sutra*.

Samanera   A novice who keeps the precepts but has not yet been ordained as a monk. (*See also* BHIKKU)

Samantabhadra   According to the AVATAMSAKA SUTRA, the greatest of all the *bodhisattvas*. The Prayer of Samantabhadra forms a devotional hymn which contains the BODHISATTA vows, often repeated in MAHAYANA forms of Buddhism. The Prayer makes the prostration fundamental to Mahayana doctrine: 'the entire universe is filled with Victorious Ones; even on the tip of a grain of sand, Buddhas as numerous as particles of dust exist, each of them sitting in the centre surrounded by *bodhisattvas*'. Typical of the vows is: 'Allow me to work to the end of time, adjusting myself to the lives of beings, fulfilling the life of enlightenment'.

Samatha   A state of concentrated calmness in which the attention is focused exclusively on a single object as a meditation aid. When the attention is fully focused SAMADHI can be achieved. Meditations which produce calmness or tranquility are contrasted with VIPASSANA where a cognitive transformation is sought.

Sambharamarga   The Path of Accumulation, which according to the BHAVANAKRAMA is the second stage in the development of a BODHISATTVA. At this stage one masters through close meditation the ability to visit celestial realms to make offerings to the Buddhas, and one is able to closely examine the body, feelings, mind and the DHAMMAS. (*See also* ASAIKSAMARGA; DARSANAMARGA; PRAYOGAMARGA)

Sambhogakaya   One of the three bodies of the Buddha according to the MAHAYANA tradition. It refers to the subtle body of bliss which appears to *bodhisattvas* when they commune with the Truth in the celestial realm. The body of bliss is material and impermanent but not corporeal in the normal sense. It is a glorified or transcendent body which sits upon the Lotus throne in a PURE LAND and preaches to the assembled *bodhisattvas*. Most Mahayana traditions claim that their SUTRAS are derived from the teachings of the sambhogakaya rather than the physical manifestation of SAKYAMUNI. (*See also* BODHISATTVA; DHAMMAKAYA; NIRMANAKAYA)

Samdinirmocana Sutra   An Indian MAHAYANA text of the CITTAMATRA tradition that claims to be the definitive and explicit rendering of the DHAMMA. It argues that the teachings of SAKYAMUNI at VARANASI on the Four Noble Truths, and his statement that all DHAMMAS lack inherent truth, require interpretation and lead to disagreement in the SANGHA. This is because they were not the definitive truth but the use of skilful means by Sakyamuni.

Samjna (S) / Sanna (P)   Perception or the awareness of sensation. The third of the five KHANDHAS or elements which make up the nature of all beings or forms of life.

Samma (P) / Samyak (S)   *Lit. supreme or true.* The summit of achievement. It can refer to the highest point that an individual can reach according to their capabilities, but it is also used to describe each step of the Noble Eightfold Path. It can also refer to the Buddha and to Enlightenment. (*See also* ARIYATTHANGIKAMAGGA; MAJJHIMA PATIPADA)

Samma ajiva   *Lit. right livelihood.* The fifth of the Eight Noble Truths, which recommends Buddhists refrain from any form of occupation that will cause harm to others, such as trading in arms, intoxicants, poisons, slaughter of animals and cheating. (*See also* ARIYATTHANGIKAMAGGA; MAJJHIMA PATIPADA)

Samma ditthi   *Lit. right understanding.* The first of the Eight Noble Truths, which refers to the understanding required to enter upon the path to enlightenment. Essentially this requires grasping the meaning and the significance of the Four Noble Truths taught by the Buddha in his first sermon at VARANASI. (*See also* ARIYATTHANGIKAMAGGA; CATTARI ARIYASACCANI; MAJJHIMA PATIPADA)

Samma kammanta   *Lit. right action.* The fourth of the Eight Noble Truths, which aims to promote correct moral and ethical conduct. It recommends abstention from dishonesty, violence, sexual misconduct and all forms of dishonourable behaviour. (*See also* ARIYATTHANGIKA-MAGGA; CATTARI ARIYASACCANI; MAJJHIMA PATIPADA)

Samma samadhi   *Lit. right concentration.* The last of the Eight Noble Truths, which is concerned with meditation in which the practitioner passes through the four stages of dhyana to the level of perfect equanimity. (*See also* ARIYATTHANGIKAMAGGA; CATTARI ARIYASACCANI; DHYANA; MAJJHIMA PATIPADA; NIRVANA; SAMADHI)

Samma sankappa   *Lit. right thought.* The second of the Eight Noble Truths, which is concerned with maintaining positive and beneficial thoughts that lead to detachment, compassion, non-violence and avoiding negative thoughts that lead to selfish desire, ill-will, hatred and anger. (*See also* ARIYATTHANGIKAMAGGA; CATTARI ARIYASACCANI; MAJJHIMA PATIPADA)

Samma sati   *Lit. right mindfulness.* The seventh of the Eight Noble Truths, which recommends to the practitioner awareness of the activities of the mind, body and sensations. Particularly associated with this is meditation upon the breath to develop self-awareness and concentration. (*See also* ARIYATTHANGIKAMAGGA; CATTARI ARIYASACCANI; KAYA; MAJJHIMA PATIPADA; VEDANA)

Samma vaca   *Lit. right speech*. The third of the Eight Noble Truths, which is concerned with abstention from telling lies and indulging in backbiting, gossip and slander that will create hatred, violence, anger or any kind of disharmony between individuals or communities. Abusive language is also shunned and generally the practitioner should maintain speech that is friendly, benevolent and promotes the DHAMMA. (*See also* ARIYATTHANGIKAMAGGA; CATTARI ARIYASACCANI; MAJJHIMA PATIPADA)

Samma vayama   *Lit. right effort*. The sixth of the Eight Noble Truths, which promotes the will to maintain the practice of the Dhamma through preventing negative states of mind from arising and encouraging the development of positive and beneficial states of mind. (*See also* ARIYATTHANGIKAMAGGA; CATTARI ARIYASACCANI; MAJJHIMA PATIPADA)

Sampanna-Krama   The adept's stage of Tantric visualization where the energies of the deity, Buddha or BODHISATTVA are absorbed into the practitioner. Ideally this is achieved after the practitioner experiences complete unity or loss of duality between himself and the chosen visualization. (*See also* TANTRA; UTPANNA-KRAMA; YIDAM)

Samsara   *Lit. continuing, becoming*. Daily life, the world of continuous flux in which all humans live, or the state of transmigration on the wheel of life in which all beings revolve, coming again and again until achieving NIRVANA. All life which is dependent upon something else for its existence or which consists of an aggregate of various components is in the realm of SAMSARA. In the Mahayana school, Nirvana and *samsara* are two aspects of one reality which is ultimate non-duality.

Samskara (S) / Sankhara (P)   The second link or NIDANA in the chain of causation and the fourth of the five KHANDHAS or elements/aggregates that make up human nature. It is used to describe the intellectual faculties or, more generally, all the contents of mind. However, in the chain of causation, the *samskaras* arise from ignorance (AVIJJA), and in, turn, give rise to consciousness (VINNANA). In this sense it applies to volitional activities which lead to the desire or longing for life. It s also used in a much more general sense to refer to all mental and physical phenomena which are conditioned or compounded. (*See also* NIDANAS)

Samudaya   The second of the Four Noble Truths taught by the Buddha in his first sermon at Sarnath near VARANASI. It is also known as TANHA. It posits that the arising or the origin of suffering lies in desire or craving. Desire itself arises from sensation and is the final chain in the wheel of causation. (*See also* DUKKHA; NIDANA; PATICCA-SAMUPPADA)

Samyak   *See* SAMMA.

Samyojana   A number of fetters that have to be broken by the successful practitioner in order to be free from suffering. There are nine altogether: belief in separate selfhood; skeptical doubt; blind attachment to rules and regulations; sexual desire; desire for physical existence; desire for celestial existence; conceit; restlessness; and ignorance. (*See also* NIBBANA; SAMSARA)

Sangha   The assembly of monks and nuns in THERAVADA but often used to denote all the community in MAHAYANA Buddhism. The order of monks was founded by Buddha, and is probably the oldest in the world. The Sangha is one of the three refuges of the Buddhist. No oaths are taken on entry to the Sangha and the BHIKKU is free to leave the Order at any time. In many Buddhist countries it is customary to enter the Sangha for a temporary retreat from the world. (*See also* BHIKKUNI)

Sanghabheda   *Lit. splitting of the Sangha.* The term used for schisms in the monastic order. It is important to remember that Buddhist schisms are not a matter of doctrine. It is possible for monks in the same monastery to hold different beliefs, since these are considered to be a personal matter. However, it is important for the same code of monastic behaviour to be observed. It is divisions over monastic discipline that lead to schism. (*See also* SANGHA)

Sankhara   *See* SAMSKARA.

Sanna   *See* SAMJNA.

Saptabuddha Sutra   A SUTRA that is devoted to the topic of the BHAISAJYAGRU, the medicine Buddha.

Saptasatika Prajnaparamita   A text, probably influenced by the meditation schools of Kashmir, that first draws upon the doctrines of infinite Buddhas to declare that one-pointed meditation upon the Buddhas' forms and remembrance of their names in a secluded place can lead to immediate and final enlightenment. This practice is named as 'Single Deed SAMADHI'.

Sarana   *Lit. protection or shelter*. Seeking the protection or refuge of the Buddha, the DHAMMA and the SANGHA. The declaration of taking the Three Refuges. (*See also* TISARANA)

Sarvastivada Vinaya   The monastic code generally adhered to by Chinese monks and available in Chinese languages. (*See also* DHARMAGUPTAKA; SARVASTIVADINS; VINAYA)

Sarvastivadins   One of the schools of early Buddhism that split away from the Sthaviravadin School around about the time of the reign of Ashoka in the third century BCE. The School dominated North Indian Buddhism for nearly a thousand years and had a profound influence on the spread of Buddhism to China. It paved the way for later MAHAYANAN doctrines of the Buddha and created the famous wheel of life consisting of the six realms of existence and the twelve-linked chain of causation. (*See also* NIDANAS)

Sasana   A term used by Theravadin Buddhists to describe the totality of Buddhism, as an occurrence in history rather than a doctrine. The present *sasana* was founded by SIDDATTHA GOTTAMA Buddha.

Sati   Mindfulness or awareness required in order to achieve success in meditation. (*See also* DHYANA; SAMMA SATI)

Satori (J)   *Lit. awakening*. The term used in ZEN Buddhism to describe a state of being where differentiation and duality are overcome. It may range from an intuitive flash or momentary experience to complete NIRVANA. It marks the beginning of the Zen path as no awareness of the reality of Zen could exist prior to *Satori*. Various Zen traditions utilize different methods to arrive at *Satori*.

Satta (P) / Sattva (S)   *Lit. being or existence*. It describes the six kinds of living being who exist in the three realms or planes of existence. (*See also* ARUPADHATU; KAMADHATU; RUPADHATU)

Satya (S)   *See* SACCA.

Sautrantika   A school of Buddhism that is an offshoot of the SARVAS-TIVADINS. However, it disagreed with the massive emphasis placed upon textual analysis of the large body of commentaries produced by the Sarvastivadins in the second century CE. The Sautrantrika denied the authority of complex manuals and treatises and closed the canon with the second of the collections, the SUTRA PITAKA. (*See also* VAIBHASIKAS)

Sesshin (J)   An intensive or extended period of ZEN meditation practice held in a RINZAI monastery. The monks can pass up to one week practising meditation in the daytime and meeting with their teacher in the evening.

Seung Sahn   (b. 1927) The founder of the Kwan Um school of Korean Buddhism famous for his teaching of the 'don't know mind'. He has opened more than fifty affiliated groups throughout Europe and Northern America.

Shakyamuni   *See* SAKYAMUNI.

Shikan taza (J)   *Lit. 'only sitting'*. A SOTO ZEN practice which refers to concentrated thought or a period of quiet reflective meditation.

Shin shu (J)   A Japanese version of PURE LAND Buddhism founded by Shinran Shonin (1173–1262) and one of the largest schools of Buddhism in Japan. It is also known as the Shin sect and it allows the marriage of priests. The Shin shu doctrine teaches that faith alone in the AMIDA Buddha is sufficient.

Shingon (J)   A sect of esoteric (*Tantric*) Buddhism introduced into Japan by Kobo Daishi (774–835). It is a syncretistic movement which believes that all the religions are the expression of self-realization towards Buddhahood. The universe is regarded as the manifestation of the ultimate reality personified in VAIROCANA Buddha.

Shinran Shonen   (1173–1262) A spiritual successor to HONEN and the founder of the JODO Shin Shu, the True PURE LAND sect. Like his master before him, Shinran taught that only faith in the AMIDA Buddha can save human beings and provide them with rebirth in the Pure Land. Faith cannot be earned but can only be given as a gift through the grace of the Buddha.

Shojo (J)   The third type of the five types of ZEN. This refers to HINAYANA or 'lesser vehicle' Zen, which is concerned with one's peace of mind. While some practitioners of the other forms of Zen acknowledge that Shojo can accommodate the inner needs of the individual, they nonetheless believe that it remains indifferent to the needs of others. In this they echo the critique of the THERAVADA school of Buddhism by the MAHAYANA.

Shraddha   The Buddhist understanding of faith. According to the ABHIDHARMAKOSA it consists of adherence to the doctrines of karma and rebirth, the Three Jewels and the Four Noble Truths. Some MAHAYANA variations add the BODHISATTVA ideal, the teachings on emptiness and the qualities of a Buddha. Faith is not considered to be unreasoned. On the contrary, Buddhist teaching asserts that on hearing a doctrine, the student should reflect rationally upon its truth. If it makes sense, only then should it be maintained.

Shunyatta / Sunyatta   The MAHAYANA concept of emptiness, based on the unreality of the chain of causation, which overcomes the delusive quality of mind that thinks of things as separate and self-sustaining. Awareness of *Shunyatta* removes delusion and helps create compassion. (*See also* KARUNA)

Siddattha Gottama (P) / Siddhartha Gautama (S) *Lit. wish-fulfilled, or, he whose purpose has been completed.* The personal name of the historical Buddha. Although there are thousands of legends told in Buddhism concerning the countless lives of the Buddha leading up to his final enlightenment, the historical figure was born in the sixth century BCE, in the small republic of Sakya, now in the modern state of Nepal. His father was the ruler of the Sakyas and according to the legend Siddattha was married at sixteen and maintained in his palace with every conceivable luxury. This was undertaken by his father, who was afraid that his son would fulfil the prophecy made at his birth to renounce the world. At the age of nineteen, after witnessing an old man, a sick person and a dead body, the young prince set out in pursuit of enlightenment and liberation from suffering. For many years he pursued a life of extreme asceticism but could not find satisfaction. Finally, he achieved enlightenment after meditating under the BODHI TREE situated in BODH-GAYA, in the modern Indian state of Bihar. The Buddha decided to teach in order to alleviate the suffering of his fellow-beings; for forty-five years he travelled across northern India in the company of his monks and nuns, teaching the practical path to release from the suffering caused by bondage to SAMSARA. (*See also* BUDDHA; CATTARI ARIYASACCANI; MAGGA; NIBBANA; SAMMA; SAKYAMUNI)

Siddha A group of wandering ascetic yogis, traditionally numbered at eighty-four, who practised Tantric rituals sometime from the ninth to twelfth centuries and followed the cult of the VAJRAYANA. They were against the formalism of the monastic orders and the ritualistic emphasis of traditional Buddhism. They were certainly influenced by converts from Hindu Tantric systems. (*See also* TANTRA)

Sila It can mean either character or habitual behaviour, or morality or moral precepts. *Sila* is embodied in the Eightfold Noble Path in the practices of right action, right speech and right effort. The ethical teachings of the Buddha were embodied in the five universal precepts binding on all Buddhists and the enlarged code of conduct for monks known as the PATIMOKKHA. The most comprehensive lisiting of moral and ethical codes is in the ten ethical precepts or *dasakusalakarmapatha*. It lists the following codes of behaviour: non-violence and compassion towards all creatures; avoidance of anything that is not given and the cultivation of generosity; abstention from sexual misconduct and contentment; maintenance of right speech; avoidance of greed and possessiveness and the cultivation of tranquility; avoidance of anger and hatred and the abandonment of false views. (*See also* PANCASILA)

Sima   The geographical boundaries of a monastery. The area confined within the boundary cannot be larger than that which is able to be walked across in order for monks to attend the UPOSATHA ceremonies each fortnight. Without the formal construction of a boundary to the community, the ceremony cannot be performed. (*See also* PATIMOKKHA)

Siyam Nikaya   The largest body of monks in Sri Lanka. However, contemporary *nikayas* are sub-divided into a number of sub-sects. The other two significant *nikayas* are the Amarapura and the Ramanna. (*See also* NIKAYA)

Skanda   *Lit. aggregate or bundle.* A technical term for the five constituents that comprise the physical mental being. They consist of RUPA, or physical being; VEDANA, or feeling; SAMJNA, or perception; SAMSKARAS, or mental activities; and VIJNANA, or consciousness. Since all these aggregates are impermanent and subject to dissolution, attachment to them will bring suffering. Their impermanence is usually taken to mean that Buddha rejected the concept of a permanent soul or ATMAN. (*See also* ANATTA; ATTA)

Skandhaka   The second part of the VINAYA PITAKA which provides the details of the rules for communal monastic life as opposed to the rules governing the behaviour of individual monks and nuns. They deal with initiation into the community, dress codes, training, retreats, resolution of disputes, and punishment for infringement of the rules. (*See also* PATIMOKKHA)

Smriti   The first of the seven stages that lead to enlightenment, it refers to mindfulness or being aware of the activities of the body, mind and sensations. It is embodied in the Noble Truth of Right Mindfulness. (*See also* PRASRABDHI; PRITI; SAMADHI; SAMMA SATI; UPEKKHA; VIRIYA)

Soka Gakkai (J)   A modern Japanese movement founded in 1931 based on the teachings of NICHIREN Buddhism (1253). Twice a day the followers chant *Namu-myoho-renge-kyo* in front of the mandala scroll originally written by Nichiren Daishonin, a thirteenth-century priest, from whom the movement gets its name. Chanting may be used to fulfil worldly desires, which may appear to be paradoxical when one considers the teachings of the Buddha. Under the name of NICHIREN SHOSHU, the school has appeared successfully in the West and attracted many young people and media stars. However, although apparently at odds with the textual warnings against desire contained in the Four Noble Truths, Nichiren is more in line with pragmatic forms of Buddhism, practised by the common people throughout the Buddhist world, where prayers and rituals are often used to fulfil personal desires for well-being. The movement actively recruits, is not ascetic and has a lay approach to Buddhism.

Soto (J)   A ZEN sect introduced into Japan by DOGEN (1200–53). It advocates ZAZEN or 'just sitting' meditation. As opposed to RINZAI, it became popular amongst the peasantry and as a result developed a number of popular rituals for rites of passage.

Sramanas   *Lit. strivers.* The term used to describe the groups of wandering ascetics such as those joined by the Buddha on his search for enlightenment. (*See also* SIDDATTHA GOTTAMA)

Srimaladevisimhanada Sutra   A third-century CE South-Indian SUTRA which teaches that the ARHANTS and PRATYEKABUDDHAS are still within the realm of KAMMA and will need to be reborn. Only the TATHAGATAGHARBA is the true domain of the Buddha and it is not comprehended or realized by non-MAHAYANAN sages and scholars.

Srotapani   The first stage on the journey to enlightenment known as 'stream-entry'. It indicates that there are only seven more births left in the human or celestial realms before NIRVANA is achieved. (*See also* ARHANT; BODHISATTVA; SAKRDAGAMIN)

Srutamayi Prajna   Wisdom or understanding that comes from discerning or interpreting the meaning of scripture as opposed to the higher wisdom that is attained by direct experience. (*See also* PANNA)

Sthavira / Sthaviravada   An early school of Buddhist tradition whose teachers considered themselves to be the strict guardians of tradition. They came into existence as a result of the first schism in Buddhist history, which took place at the Second Council between fifty and one hundred years after the Buddha's death. The creation of Sthavira and MAHASANGHITA schools began the basic division in Buddhism between MAHAYANA and THERAVADA. However, it should be remembered that the contemporary Theravadin School was not Sthavira but one of several schools that came into existence resulting from divisions within the Sthavira. (*See also* SARVASTIVADIN)

Stupa (S) / Thupa (P)   A reliquary mound containing the ashes or relics of an important religious personage or monuments commemorating events in the life of the Buddha. They are dome shaped and constructed on a rectangular platform. Some of them are extremely large whilst others are very small.

Subha   *Lit. beautiful, or, that which is beautiful.* Some Buddhists believe that a momentary enlightenment can be achieved through loss of self, attained by an appreciation of beauty or contemplation of great beauty. The Buddha did not deny the beauty of the world but was aware that attachment to the ephemeral would result in eventual suffering. (*See also* DUKKHA)

Suddhodana   The ruler of the Sakya tribe and the father of SIDDATTHA GOTTAMA, the future Buddha. It is Suddhodana who tried to prevent his son from experiencing any suffering by creating a palace of luxury for the young prince. The intention was to avoid a prophecy in which his son would renounce the world to become a wandering ascetic.

Sujata   The milkmaid who nourished the Buddha back to health after he had failed to find enlightenment through the practice of extreme austerity. According to some accounts of the legend, she was the first to introduce him to the idea of the middle way by providing the example of a sitar string that is either too loose or too tight. (*See also* SIDDATTHA GOTTAMA; MAGGA)

Sukhavati   Paradise as described by PURE LAND Buddhists of the JODO and SHIN Schools in Japan. It is the 'Pure Land' of the AMIDA Buddha.

Sukhavativyuha Sutra   A second-century CE sutra translated into Chinese in 402 CE. The original is known as the Larger and the translation as the Smaller. Although the Japanese believe the Smaller to be the original. Both versions are devoted to the AMIDA Buddha whose radiance is described as illuminating all the Buddha realms. The Larger speaks of the BODHISATTVA DHAMMAKAYA who makes a vow to create a Buddha realm that exceeds all others. Since this was achieved by Amida, it is understood by PURE LAND Buddhists that Dhammakaya was an earlier incarnation of Amida.

Sukhavativyuhopadesha   A work of unknown authorship influential in the development of PURE LAND Buddhism in China. The text expounds on the meaning of faith in the AMIDA Buddha and explains that birth in the Pure Land is not for reward but to obtain enlightenment and then teach to all sentient beings out of compassion.

Sunna (P) / Sunya (S)   The emptiness of all existence or the doctrine that nothing exists in itself, as taught by some early schools of Buddhism. It means the Void of Emptiness and implies the denial of all conceptual constructions in relation to ultimate reality. (*See also* SHUNYATTA)

Suryaprabha   A BODHISATTVA who attends the Medicine Buddha and brings the dead into his presence. (*See also* BHAISAJYAGURU)

Sutra (S) / Sutta (P)   *Lit. a thread.* A collection of aphorisms on a single theme. A common form of Buddhist scripture which is written in the form of a dialogue or discourse between the Buddha and a disciple or seeker. (*See also* SUTTA PITAKA)

Sutta Pitaka (P) / Sutra Pitaka (S)   The second of the three baskets of scripture in the PALI CANON which contains the dialogues or discourses of the Buddha. There are over 17,000 *sutras* that describe the teaching output of the Buddha over forty-five years. Each SUTRA has an introduction which describes the circumstances in the Buddha's life which preceded the teaching. They are all introduced by the testimony of Buddha'a closest disciple, Ananda, reassuring the adherent that he was a witness to the event. However, many of the *sutras* were certainly compiled after the Buddha's death. (*See also* TIPITAKA)

Sutta-vibhanga (P)   The portion of the VINAYA PITAKA which provides explanatory commentaries on the monastic rule, organizes offences into categories, and prescribes the appropriate punishment. (*See also* KHANDHAKA)

Svabhavikakaya   The essence body of the Buddha, a non-dualistic perfect flow of consciousness that is the true nature of the Buddhas. It is the same as the DHAMMAKAYA, but the latter term refers to its role as the sustainer of all the DHAMMAS. (*See also* TRIKAYA)

Svatantrika   A sub-division of the MADHYAMAKA believed to have been founded by Bhavaviveka (500–70), an opponent of Buddhapalita (470–540), the originator of the PRASANGIKA school. The division seemed to be one of methodology. The Svatantrika posited that arguments challenging the doctrine of absolute reality or independent existence must follow the logical structure recognized by other Indian schools of thought. The two sub-divisions were to take on significance in Tibet where their arguments over methodology remain a significant part of Buddhist education.

T

Tanha (P) / Trishna (S)   The Second of the Four Noble Truths taught by
the Buddha in his first sermon at Sarnath. Having first identified
DUKKHA or suffering as the first Noble Truth, the Buddha explains that
Dukkha has a cause variously translated as thirst, craving, or desire.
Tanha or the thirst for life is also one of the *nidanas* or links in the
chain of causation. It depends on VEDANA and, in turn, is depended
upon by UPADANA. (*See also* SAMUDAYA)

Tantra   A form of MAHAYANA Buddhism which spread from India to Tibet
and then to China. Tibetan Tantric texts are believed to have been
revealed by the Buddha as an elite esoteric discipline available only to
initiates. The practitioner of TANTRA must have a qualified teacher who
initiates the disciple into various practices for the attainment of
Buddhahood. Traditionally these involved the use of *mantras* and
mandalas for aid in meditation. However, the Tantric scriptures are
believed to be magical. They contain spells, descriptions of divinities
and instructions concerning ritual. (*See also* DHARANA; MANTRA)

Tara   A Tibetan female BODHISATTVA whose veneration is widespread in
Western Buddhist centres. She is associated with Avalokiteshwara
and is said to have been born from a tear that he wept out of
compassion for the endless numbers of sentient beings who needed to
be saved. She came into existence to assist Avalokiteshwara, but is
often regarded in Tibet as a fully enlightened female Buddha. She is
generally represented as either a white or green young woman, either
sitting in the lotus position or upon a moon resting on a lotus.

Tara Tantra   A text which extols TARA, referring to her as the Mother of all the Buddhas.

Tariki (J)   Reliance on powers outside oneself or seeking salvation from outside assistance. Used by PURE LAND Buddhists to describe salvation through faith and devotion to the personification of the absolute manifested in the AMIDA Buddha. (*See also* JIRIKI; JODO; SOTO)

Tathagata (S)   A title to describe the Buddha used by both his followers and himself. The meaning is probably something like 'one who has arrived' or 'one who has realized suchness' (TATHAHA). Other interpretations suggest that it means 'one who has come and gone'. (*See also* BUDDHA)

Tathagatagarbha   A tradition in MAHAYANA Buddhism that is concerned with the Buddha nature and the tension between the idea of becoming enlightened and the reality that all things already share in the Buddha nature as their deepest reality. Without the presence of the Buddha nature (the tathagatagarbha) there would be no tendency within the human being to seek enlightenment.

Tathagatagarbha Sutra   The SUTRA that asserts that all beings have within them a fully enlightened Buddha. (*See also* MAHAPARINIRVANA SUTRA)

Tathaha (S)   *Lit. suchness.* Used by MAHAYANA Buddhists to describe the ultimate and unconditioned nature of all things. It has to be found on the path to enlightenment, but it cannot be discovered by searching for it, nor can it be lost, as one is never separate from it. (*See also* DHAMMAKAYA; SHUNYATA; SUNYA)

Tendai (J)   A syncretic school of Buddhism introduced into Japan from China by SAICHO (767–822). It considers the Lotus Sutra to be the ultimate and final teachings of the Buddha. (*See also* TI'EN TAI)

Thang-ka (T)   Hanging scrolls that contain MANDALAS, often depicting the wheel of existence and a variety of BODHISATTVAS, painted according to precise formulas and used in Tantric visualization disciplines. (*See also* SAMPANNA KARMA; TANTRA; UTPANNA-KRAMA)

Theravada (P)   *Lit. way of the elders.* A principal school of Buddhism established by Mahinda in around 247 BCE in Sri Lanka and South-East Asia as a result of a mission dispatched by Asoka. Originally a sub-sect of the dominant STHAVIRA School, its form of Buddhism gradually prevailed. Today, the THERAVADA School is the only remaining school of the original eighteen HINAYANA Schools. It claims to preserve the Buddha's teachings in their pure form transmitted through the collection of scripture known as the PALI CANON. (*See also* MAHAYANA)

Theravada Vinaya   The monastic code of the Theravadin schools. They possess the only VINAYA written in the original language of Pali, used in Sri Lanka and South-East Asia. (*See also* THERAVADA)

Thupa (P)   *See* STUPA.

Ti'en T'ai (Ch)   Chinese School of Buddhism founded by Chih-i (538–97), which was introduced into Japan where it is known as TENDAI. It gives ultimate status to the LOTUS SUTRA and teaches that all things partake of a single organic unity. Therefore all things partake of the Buddha nature as they are manifestations of the One Mind.

Tipitaka (P) / Tripitaka (S)   *Lit. the three baskets.* The PALI CANON of Buddhist scriptures accepted by the THERAVADA School. It is divided into three main parts consisting of the VINAYA PITAKA, SUTTA PITAKA and ABIDHAMMA PITAKA.

Tiratana (P) / Tisatana (P) / Triratna (S)   The triple refuge in the Buddha, the DHAMMA and the SANGHA which is referred to as the Three Jewels and is the foundation of Buddhism. Swearing allegiance or faith in the Three Refuges is the initiation into becoming a Buddhist. (*See also* BUDDHA; SARANA)

Tisarana (P) / Trisarana (S)   A technical term for the 'Three Refuges' that refers to the actual vow made in the ceremony in which one formally agrees to become a Buddhist. It involves repeating 'I go to refuge in the Buddha, I go to refuge in the DHAMMA, I go to refuge in the Sangha' three times. (*See also* BUDDHA; SARANA; TIRATANA)

Ti-Tsang pen-ying Ching (Ch)   A SUTRA of Chinese origin recited on behalf of ancestors, before the birth of a child and to secure family members from disease. The *sutra* recounts the deeds and powers of the BODHISATTVA KSITIGARBHA.

Trikaya (P) / Tripikaya (S)   The MAHAYANA doctrine of the three bodies of the Buddha or aspects of Buddha nature. They are (i) the eternal teaching or essence (ii) the historical Buddha (iii) the transcendental Buddha. (*See also* DHAMMAKAYA; NIRMANAKAYA; SAMBHOGAKAYA)

Tulku (T)   *Lit. emanation.* A term used in several ways by Tibetan Buddhism: (i) reincarnated Lama who is found by a rigorous process of recognition as a small child and raised to fulfil the function they were believed to have performed in their last life; (ii) the appearance in the world of a Buddha who has refused NIRVANA in order to assist suffering beings; (iii) the use of a human body by a spiritual power. (*See also* BODDHISATTVA; DALAI LAMA; NIRMANAKAYA; PANCHEN LAMA)

Tusita   A heavenly realm close to the Earth where the future Buddha named MAITREYA awaits rebirth.

U

Upadana   The ninth NIDANA or link in the chain of causation which maintains the wheel of SAMSARA. It refers to attachment or clinging to life. It depends on TANHA and gives rise to BHAVA.

Upasaka (M) / Upasika (F)   Buddhists who maintain the five precepts at all times whilst living in the world rather than retiring to a monastery or convent. (*See also* PANCASILA)

Upasampada   The more formal or higher ordination ceremony for a monk which cannot take place until the postulant is twenty years old. He is presented by the monk who has become his teacher to a formal assembly of monks and questioned. (*See also* PABBAJJA; PATIMOKKHA; SAMANERA)

Upaya   *Lit. skilful means.* In Mahayana Buddhism it refers to a practical means to achieve a spiritual goal. However, once the goal has been achieved the means should be put aside to avoid attachment. It is sometimes used to refer to any meditation on loving awareness in order to overcome anger. (*See also* BHAVANA)

Upayakausalya Sutra   A SUTRA composed of questions and answers concerning legendary events which demonstrate that they were a form of skilfil means to serve the purposes of the teaching of the DHAMMA. (*See also* UPAYA)

Upekkha (P) / Upeksa (S)   The BRAHMA VIHARA of equanimity or complete evenness of mind in the face of all the diversity of experience.

Uposatha   Certain days of the month which are based on the lunar cycle, generally the full and new moon. From early times they were recognized by the SANGHA (community of monks) to participate in special events like expounding or listening to the DHAMMA or maintaining fasts. Most Buddhist countries still uphold them and they are utilized by monks for fasting or public confession. The repetition of the 227 precepts that takes place every fornight in THERAVADA monastic communities is also known as the UPOSATHA ceremony as it coincides with the lunar cycle. (*See also* PATIMOKKHA)

Utpanna-krama   The first stage of Tantric visualization practices where the practitioner becomes familiar with the *mandala* and the characteristics of the deity, Buddha or bodhisattva until it becomes a living being. (*See also* TANTRA; SAMPANNA-KRAMA)

V

Vaibhasikas   One of two divisions of the SARVASTIVADINS. The Vaibhasikas acknowledged the authority of the large body of treatises, manuals and commentaries produced by the Sarvastivadins in the second century CE. From its stronghold in Kashmir it came to have a considerable influence on Buddhist scholasticism and the emphasis on the ABHIDHARMA in THERAVADA circles. (*See also* SAUTRANTIKA)

Vairocana   The Great Illumination Buddha of the AVATAMSAKA SUTRA, who does not teach but rather approves of the preaching of his countless retinue of *bodhisattvas*. He is a cosmic Buddha who contains within himself all other Buddhas, *bodhisattvas* and universes. (*See also* BODHISATTVA)

Vaisakha (S) / Vesakha (P)   *See* WESAK.

Vajja (P) / Vrajya (S)   Actions which produce bad results and should therefore be avoided in order to avoid the consequences which could result in an undesirable rebirth. (*See also* KAMMA; SAMSARA)

Vajracchedika   The famous Diamond SUTRA, known as the *Perfection of Wisdom*, a Tantric text used by the VAJRAYANA. (*See also* TANTRA)

Vajrayana   *Lit. diamond vehicle.* A distinct teaching, esoteric in nature, which originated between the third and seventh centuries CE in India and Tibet. It is more commonly known as TANTRA. The name derives from the deity Vajrayana (the adamantine vehicle) which utilizes the symbol of the thunderbolt, the weapon used by the Indian god Indra. The tradition is heavily dependent on the use of mantra and borrows heavily from Shaivite traditions in which sexual union is the paradigm for spiritual union. Emptiness and bliss in union and loss of self become the practitioner's goal. (*See also* SIDDHA; TANTRA)

Varanasi   Although the most sacred of the Hindu pilgrimage cities, Varanasi is also famous for the delivery of the first sermon of the Buddha after he attained enlightenment, in which he spoke of the Four Noble Truths and Noble Eightfold Path. The city still contains the deerpark of Sarnath, a Buddhist pilgrimage centre said to be the site of the sermon and one of the locations for an offshoot of the BODHI TREE.

Vedana   Sense perception or feeling. It is the second of the five KHANDHAS which make up life on the material plane. It is also the seventh link or NIDANA in the chain of causation dependent on PHASSA and giving rise to TANHA.

Vesak / Vesakha / Vesakka   *See* WESAK.

Vibhajja-vadin   *Lit. analysts.* A self-definition given by Theravadins to differentiate themselves from other Buddhists. It refers to their delight in analyzing psychological states and is reflective of the contents of the ABHIDHAMMA PITAKA. (*See also* THERAVADA)

Vihara   *Lit. a dwelling place.* Originally used to describe houses that were donated to the Buddha for his use, it is now used as a term for a monastery or place of retreat. It can also be used to describe a stage in the spiritual life. (*See also* BRAHMA VIHARA)

Vimalakakirtinirdesa Sutra   A SUTRA used by MAHAYANA traditions to support their doctrines concerning the significance of the Buddhist laity and their ability to attain the same levels of enlightenment as the monks. The *sutra* demonstrates this doctrinal position by presenting the layman Vimalakirti as an advanced BODHISATTVA, capable of communicating philosophical concepts, but significantly upbraiding and correcting a number of the Buddha's principal monastic followers (*See also* ASOKADATTAVYAKARANA SUTRA; BHADRAMAYAKARAVYAKARANA SUTRA)

Vinaya   The list of rules and regulations governing the life of monks and nuns contained in the first basket of scriptures in the PALI CANON. These were adopted by MAHAYANA and THERAVADA orders of monks as the Pali Canon contained the only surviving complete Vinaya. (*See also* MULASARVASTIVADA; SARVASTIVADA; VINAYA PITAKA)

Vinaya Pitaka   The first of the three baskets of scriptures that form the TIPITAKA. They contain rules for establishing and governing the SANGHA. In these can be found the regulations governing the lives of monks and nuns. (*See also* ABHIDHAMMA PITAKA; PATIMOKKHA; PITAKA; SUTTA PITAKA; TIPITAKA)

Vinnana (P) / Vijnana (S)   Individual consciousness or conscious thought. It is the fifth of the five KHANDHAS which make up life on the material plane. It also refers to the third link or NIDANA in the chain of causation which is dependent upon the SANKHARAS and gives rise to NAMA RUPA.

Vinnanahara   *Lit. consciousness*. One of the four causes or conditions which are believed to be essential for the existence and continuity of all beings. (*See also* AHARA)

Vipassana (P) / Vipashyana (S)   Insight into the true nature of things. Also used to describe certain forms of meditation used by Buddhists that achieve such insight. It is *Vipassana* that leads to the realization of the Ultimate Truth or NIRVANA. In *Vipassana* meditation, which could be described as uniquely Buddhist, the practitioner focuses on achieving an insightful awareness of the processes of ANITYA, ANATMAN, and DUKKHA that form the essence of SAMSARA. (*See also* DHYANA)

Viriya (P) / Virya (S)   Energy or exertion applied to the practice of the DHAMMA which corresponds to the Noble Truth of Right Effort. One of the six virtues necessary to attain Buddhahood. (*See also* PARAMI; SAMMA VAYAMA)

Visuddhi-magga   *Lit. the path to purity.* An important contribution to the sacred literature of the THERAVADA Canon. Although it is only one of the ancillary texts that support the ABHIDHAMMA PITAKA, it provides a comprehensive and momumental summary of Theravadin doctrine. It was written in Ceylon in the early part of the fifth century CE by the monk BUDDHAGHOSA.

Vrajya (S)   *See* VAJJA.

Wesak   Buddha Day. The Sinhalese name of the festival held on the full moon of the month between April and May, which celebrates the birth, death and enlightenment of the Buddha. Japanese ZEN schools only celebrate the birth of the Buddha on 8 April.

Y

Yama The Lord of Death, and the Judge who weighs the *karmic* actions.

Yana A term used to refer to the Way or Path. Although it can refer to the teachings of the Buddha, it is more commonly used to mean a vehicle, that is a way to enlightenment, such as a particular school of Buddhism.

Yantra (S) A mystical diagram conceived in meditation and used to aid concentration in Tibetan Buddhism. A *Yantra* is seen whereas MANTRA is spoken or TANTRA is performed.

Yatha bhuta jnana darsana *Lit. seeing things as they really are.* A phrase that is repeated many times in Buddhist SUTRAS and functions as a short-hand description of the Buddha's insight and the ultimate goal of the practising Buddhist adherent.

Yidam A personal deity matched to the disciple's nature or psychological profile used in the VAJRAYANA tradition of Buddhism as a visualization in meditation. They can be male or female and possessed of a number of different qualities which are matched to the disciple's spiritual needs. They are believed to be manifestations of the SAMBHOGAKAYA.

Yogacara A school of philosophy founded by ASANGA (310–90) who is believed to have received the teachings direct from MAITREYA, the future Buddha. It propounds the idea that only consciousness is real and emphasizes the practice of meditation. (*See also* CITTAMATRA)

Z

Zazen (J)   *Lit. Zen sitting.* ZEN Buddhist forms of sitting meditation usually practised in the Lotus position. The meditation sessions normally take place in the ZENDO. (*See also* SESSHIN)

Zen (J)   A type of MAHAYANA Buddhism developed in China, where it is known as CH'AN, and then transported to Japan. It emphasizes meditation, direct experience, and enlightenment without dependence on scriptures or external authority, although usually a master is required. The essence of zen is described in the famous words attributed to its founder BODHIDHARMA as: *A special transmission outside of the scriptures; no dependence on words or letters; direct pointing to the soul of man; seeing into one's nature, and the attainment of Buddhahood.* The term is derived from the Sanskrit DHYANA meaning intense or ecstatic concentration, although it is important to acknowledge that the path of Zen is about realizing the Buddha nature in everyday life. In order to accomplish this goal there are several different schools of Zen Buddhism.

Zendo (J)   A hall usually in a separate building within the grounds of a monastery used by ZEN Buddhist monks for meditation and sleeping. (*See also* ZAZEN)

Zenga (J)   Ink drawings which indicate the spirit of ZEN by attempting to capture the essence of the eternal now.

Zenji (J) The title of respect used for a teacher of ZEN. Zen Buddhism considers that the guidance of an enlightened master is an essential requirement to attain realization of the Buddha nature.